SPONTANEOUS PLAY
IN EARLY CHILDHOOD

E.C.E. PROGRAM

SPONTANEOUS PLAY IN EARLY CHILDHOOD

M.C. Pugmire-Stoy

DELMAR PUBLISHERS INC.®

NOTICE TO THE READER

Cover art by Dahl Taylor

Delmar staff
Senior Administrative Editor: Jay Whitney
Project Editor: Carol Micheli
Production Supervisor: Larry Main
Art Coordinator: John Lent
Senior Design Supervisor: Susan C. Mathews

For information, address Delmar Publishers Inc.
2 Computer Drive, West, Box 15-015,
Albany, NY   12212-9985

Printed in the United States of America
Published simultaneously in Canada
by Nelson Canada,
a division of The Thomson Corporation

10   9   8   7   6   5   4   3   2   1

Library of Congress Cataloging-in-Publication Data
Pugmire-Stoy, M.C. (Mary Carolyn)
    Spontaneous play / M.C. Pugmire-Stoy
        p.   cm.
    Includes bibliographical references (p.) and index.
    ISBN 0-8273-3660-8
    1. Play. 2. Child development..   I. Title.
HQ782.P84 1992
    155.4 ' 18—dc20
                                                                    91-12150
                                                                    CIP

Contents

To Ricks College
Rexburg, Idaho
where my work and PLAY
have enabled me
to learn about living more effectively

Introduction

COME! READ! INTERACT! BE PLAYFUL AS YOU LEARN ABOUT PLAY!

A book on play should present relevant material on play in a logical, effective manner—this text does. But there should be a playful element, too. this has been my aim because I believe everyone learns more about living when there is a ludic (PLAYFUL) approach to at least part of the subject matter.

I have created a framework of play called "Play: The Vehicle for a Child to Learn About Living," Figure 1-1, page 1. Go ahead. Take a look!

This "vehicle" has been made into an illustration that shows the four divisions of play as "wheels" on a car. This Vehicle of Play will help you:

- Learn the basics about play, particularly spontaneous play
- Learn to observe children at play more effectively
- Look at pictures (there are 200 meaningful ones in this text) and be able to tell what the children are learning and/or how they are growing through play
- Do the same with frames from a videotape (Hopefully the tape can be made of your children
- Gain an understanding that young handi-capable children can learn about living through play experiences, too
- Have an enjoyable time studying about PLAY!

The book is divided into four sections. All of the sections are based on the Framework of Play, "Play: The Vehicle for a Child to Learn About Living.

Section 1 deals with definitions relating to play and children's work. The Framework of Play—social dimensions, types, elements, and provisions for play—is presented. A way for the student to be involved with the illustrations is given; the illustrations are an integral part of the text. An observation form based on the Framework of Play is presented. These learning devices have been thoroughly field tested.

Section 2 deals with ages and stages in the development of the child. The section also shows with pictures and captions how children's play develops. Again, spontaneous play is emphasized. A plan is presented to help the caregiver guide play in a way that lets the child be in the "driver's seat."

Section 3 provides outlines of some particularly significant play sequences, such as ball and block play. Because the development of communication skills is so vital to the child's development, a sequence of language development as it relates to play is given.

Section 4 deals with the play of special needs children. Text and pictures show that the basic Framework of Play can be used with children with handicapping conditions.

Applications for caregivers are featured in all four sections in order that the reader of this book may apply the knowledge immediately in his/her work and play with children. Particularly helpful is a plan to help adults guide *handi-capable children* in their play so that each child can take control of his/her own activities.

Observations using the "Vehicle of Play Framework" are featured. Through meaningful observations, almost every student of children's play can gain more insight into the ways children learn about living.

Almost all of the illustrations were taken in unrehearsed and informal situations in homes and various types of early childhood education centers and playgrounds. Actual ages at the time of photographing are recorded underneath the illustrations. They are not necessarily the earliest ages at which the indicated play/work abilities appear.

This text can be used for a one credit college course. It is written with the idea of being used in the student's particular situation, e.g. day care, preschool, a parent taking care of a child. It can also be used as a supplement to a child development course, part of a "core" course in early childhood education or the basis for a seminar on play. Those working with implementation of PL 99–457 will find insight about play and development as they work with families of young handicapped children.

A portion of the text is based on the work of Dr. Mary Sheridan, an English pediatrician who practiced medicine for forty years, beginning in 1937. Dr. Sheridan was interested in the main varieties of spontaneous play that engage the active interest of normal children and some of the more obvious implications for the understanding and encouragement of the play needs of handicapped children in corresponding phases of development.

The author (Pugmire-Stoy) has been actively engaged in early childhood education since the 1950s. This includes graduating from Brigham Young University (B.A.) and Idaho State University (M.A.ED). I have also attended several other universities and have studied early childhood centers in England, Wales, and Japan. My teaching includes toddler playgroups, nursery school, kindergarten, Project Head Start (including the pilot project in 1965), second grade, and "specialized" teaching in handicapped groups. I have taught in college and university settings since 1964. Needless to say, I have been involved in academic research, both as a graduate student and as an involved participant in child development centers. I have worked on a statewide developmental disability commission and am currently officially working in my state to implement the birth to three provisions of PL 99–457, the 1987 law that will give aid to the very young and will necessitate workers trained in new ways. Also, I have raised four children. I been a "traditional" mother, a single mother, and a stepmother; I am a grandmother of seven grandchildren and a "pseudo-grandmother" to four others—all of them being great players!

I have had six other books published as well as several articles. I am involved in research on play using videotapes to help parents realize how much their children are learning about living through play experiences.

Currently I am Chair of the Department of Family Science at Ricks College. Ricks College in Rexburg, Idaho, is the largest private junior college in the United States. Ricks is unique in the fact that we have approximately fifteen hundred students a year who study basic child development. We have also developed our own model of teacher training for early childhood specialists. Learning through play is a solid component of that model. Our labs are accredited by the National Association for the Education of Young Children. (Of course, I am active in that professional organization. I am a validator for the National Academy.) Other organization are: Eastern Idaho Association for the Education of Young Children, the Idaho Parents [Professionals] UnLimited (IPUL), and Soroptimist, International.

Acknowledgments

The author wishes to express her appreciation to the following individuals and agencies:

Charles Stoy, husband, and my children David and Patty Pugmire, Paul and Nancy Pugmire, Carrie and Brent Gifford, and Merrill Pugmire — thanks for the great support

Other family members, particularly our grandchildren Preston, McKay, Daniel, Melanie, Andrew, Matthew, and Kyle, and nieces and nephews Kristen, Lee Ann, Selma, Sierra Dawn, Laurie, Lauretta, Jalah, Danita, and Carl

"Almost" family members, Jenny Moser Anderson (illustrator), Kathie Price (colleague and photographer) and children Julie, Jason, Bryan, Stacy, and Sheila Mitchell

Nancy Nielson, photographer; John, Andrea, Ruth, Leah, Sarah, and Diane Nielson

Ricks College Lab Schools, Rexburg, Idaho — Helen Lindsay, Director; parents and particularly the preschoolers, the toddlers, and the handi-capable children

David Duerden, colleague and advisor. All the members of the Department of Family Science, Ricks College, and Department members' children — Jacob, Jeff, Camie, Hilary, Marie, and Jessica

The students in Ricks College's AA Degree Program in Professional Preschool Education, Dept. of Family Science

Marlaine B. Davis and Annjeanette G. Anderson for pilot testing the first class

Omega Head Start, Phoenix, Arizona — Theresa Anderson, Supervisor

Joe Hamilton State Preschool, Crescent City, California — Marsha Johnson, Teacher

Walton Day Care and Foster Home, Idaho Falls, Idaho — Margaret and Alf Walton, foster parents and our hero and heroine! Thanks to the children, too.

Sixth Ward, Church of Jesus Christ of Latter Day Saints, Rexburg, Idaho — Nursery and homes. Thanks neighbors!

Region Seven, Health and Welfare personnel; Adult/Child Development Center — Val Denton Supervisor

Toys-R-Us, Phoenix, Arizona, Stores. Thanks for the cooperation.

Idaho Parents [Professionals] Unlimited (IPUL), Parents and children, Boise, Idaho

Jason and Marianne Birch, Margaret and Hannah Bake, Coleen and Patricia Roundy, Randy Batton and family, Lindsay Bean and family. Your lives inspire others!

Progressive Day School, Idaho Falls, Idaho — Jana Jones, Owner and Director

Pugmire Daycare Home, Phoenix, Arizona — Nancy Pugmire, Director

Hibbard School Special Education Unit, Rexburg, Idaho — Sue Haroldson-Smith, Teacher

Dr. Ralph McBride, photographer, and Joyce McBride, for their support

Dr. Veryl Larsen, photographer, Lakewood, Colorado

Delmar Photographic Division

The author wishes to thank NFER-NELSON for their cooperation with this adaptation of *Spontaneous Play* by Mary D. Sheridan.

In addition special appreciation is due to the reviewers involved in the development of the text:

Tanya Collins
McDowellTech. Community College
Marion, NC

Dorace Jeanne Goodwin
Brainerd Community College
Brainerd, MN

Faye Murphy
Tarrant County Community College
Ft. Worth, TX

Susan Nalbone
University of Northern Colorado
Greeley, CO

Rebecca Reid
SUNY — Cobleskill
Cobleskill, NY

Play: A Vehicle for Learning About Living

THOUGHT QUESTIONS

- Why does the Framework of Play have four parts plus? Aren't the "old" categorizations enough?
- Why should there be a concern about play for special needs children?
- Why do so many parents/caregivers refer to play as "JUSTplay" (as though it were one word)?

PLAY: A VEHICLE FOR LEARNING ABOUT LIVING!

The child who is playing is in the driver's seat. As the "driver," the child controls the vehicle through his/her own actions. The child maneuvers the vehicle best when the four "wheels" are working well together. These four wheels represent the *social* dimensions of play, the *types* of play (cognitive; developmental), the *elements* of play that lead to further growth, and the *provisions* for play. These wheels keep the vehicle balanced so that the child is able to "turn the corners and take the bumps of life" smoothly. Every child wants his/her own individual vehicle of play and each one deserves it! That is what this book is all about. (This Vehicle of Play is pictured in Figure 1-1 and will be referred to throughout the text.)

Comparing play to a four-wheeled vehicle being driven by the child can help any person who works with children understand the importance and the scope of play. This simple device can serve as a framework that readers can use to retain the knowledge which has been gained through formal research as well as valuable information acquired by field workers. As mentioned in the Introduction, one of those field workers is a pediatrician, Dr. Mary Sheridan, who worked in England for over forty years and whose work and observations are often referred to in this book. Another field worker is your author, M.C. Pugmire-Stoy. I have been engaged in some phase of professional early childhood education since 1954.

Dr. Sheridan made it clear that she wrote as a practical pediatrician and educationist, not as an experimental psychologist. Her professional inquiries during forty years of practice were conducted at field level and directed towards producing some urgently needed clinical testing procedure which provided appropriate guidelines for treatment. Empirical

1

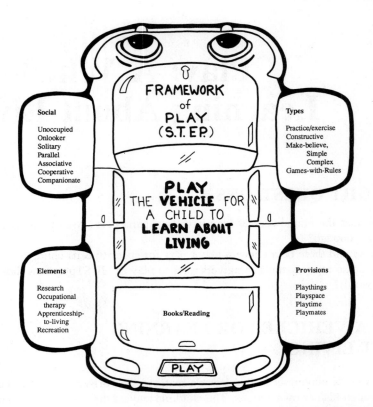

Figure 1-1   The Framework of Play. A vehicle for the child to learn about living. This is the basis for the content of this book. The four wheels of the vehicle represent the Social dimension of play, the Types of play, the Elements of play that lead to growth, and the Provisions for play. *(Courtesy of Jenny Moser-Anderson, Illustrator)*

observational research of the sort she conducted was not founded in structured situations, controlled sampling, and computer analysis. Although she recognized the value of such studies for other purposes, she felt that her long experience in hospitals, clinics, nurseries, and every type of school taught her that the most detailed study of the work of learned theorists often did not provide understanding of real children in everyday situations. She stressed the fact that there is no short-cut to clinical expertise. The only sure way to learn how to identify, assess, and guide exceptional children in the earliest stage of deviance is to begin by acquiring factual knowledge of the nature and range of normal development. It was during her studies of the early development of vision, hearing, and language that she came to slowly appreciate the need to consider the full pediatric and educational implications of the SPONTANEOUS PLAY of very young normal children and, even more pertinently, the play of young, pre-verbal handicapped children.

Some people disagree with Dr. Sheridan because so much has been learned about real children from the "detailed study of the work of learned theorists." However, I, along with others, have found that Dr. Sheridan's work gives great insight into the nature of children and how they develop and learn.

Sheridan noted that she was obliged to go out and look for herself since smaller video-taping cameras were only available in the later part of her intense observing (the early and middle seventies). She noted behavioral details during the course of her ordinary work. Only much later did she realize that what she later termed "fringe observation" was most valuable to her particular purposes since the behavior of everyone concerned, herself included, was entirely natural. There was often considerable difference between the abilities a child registered under laboratory conditions and those spontaneously demonstrated in more naturalistic circumstances.

Using the knowledge gained about young children in natural settings is vital if we are to effectively guide children so that they can lead well-rounded, productive lives. I agree with Dr. Sheridan on that point. However, the research of the past few years has revealed much to us. Therefore the facts presented in this book have been compared to the latest available research and the reader will have the benefit of both approaches.

EACH CHILD AS A PLAYER

Every child has the right to be cherished as an individual and encouraged to develop at his/her own pace, within the affection and security of his/her own family and the friendly acceptance of neighbors. Young, handicapped children have a special need for the constant, taken-for-granted, physical, mental, emotional, and social stimulation that comes from being handled, talked to, applauded, and played with and that are inherent in ordinary good child care. Since they are often demanding of attention, however, their parents, teachers, and other caregivers require special guidance in their day-to-day management; in keeping them healthy and contented; and in training them to move about safely, occupy themselves profitably, and communicate effectively with others.

In common with all the young of the earth, children learn the basic rules of species behavior, that is, the special life-style of human beings, from observation and imitation of their parents and caregivers. However, human children alone are actively instructed extensively by their elders over a long period of time. A child's integrations into the social world is founded on two dominant inborn drives: to establish rewarding personal relationships, and to learn essential everyday skills through play. In play, a child accomplishes many things:

- experiments with people and things
- stores information in his/her memory
- studies causes and effects
- reasons out problems
- builds a useful vocabulary
- learns to control self-centered emotional reactions and impulses
- adapts behaviors to the cultural habits of his/her social group
- interprets new and, on occasion, stressful events
- increases positive ideas about self-concept
- develops fine and gross motor skills

Play is as necessary to a child's full development of body, intellect, and personality as are food, shelter, clothing, fresh air, exercise, rest, and the prevention of illness and accidents to his/her continued effective existence as a human being.

Part of the activities of young childhood that many have formerly called "JUSTplay" are actually the work of learning to live in this world. Activities such as learning to hold a crayon or pencil, to take turns, to share, to work cooperatively, etc., are viewed repeatedly as children are observed in spontaneous involvement in various settings.

Provision of suitable playthings, playspace, playtime, and playmates for all young children and particularly for young handicapped children who cannot assist themselves in certain tasks, is therefore of primary importance.

DEFINITIONS

Play has been defined in many and varied ways, but a common agreement is that the child must have control over the actions in order for true play to occur, particularly spontaneous play. Therefore, the following definition will be used to guide the contents of this text:

PLAY IS THE EAGER ENGAGEMENT IN PLEASURABLE PHYSICAL OR MENTAL EFFORT TO OBTAIN EMOTIONAL SATISFACTION. THE PLAYER MUST HAVE CONTROL OF THE ACTIONS.

- *Spontaneous work* is the voluntary engagement in disciplined physical or mental effort to obtain material benefit or desired reward/praise. Some encouragement/advice by significant others may be present, but it is offered at the child's request and is not forced on the child.
- *Drudgery* is the enforced engagement in distasteful physical or mental effort to obtain the means of survival.
- *PLOY* is a word created by Dr. Mary Sheridan to designate the merging of play and work. She used the term, *SLOG*, to indicate the merging of work and drudgery. Sheridan emphasized the fact that play and work often merge in meaningful ways, but play and drudgery do not merge!

The everyday world of school children provides a foretaste of the adult world in that their daily work consists of uneven and fluctuating combinations of *ploy* (acquired competence), and *slog*. This is similar to our own work which consists of varying amounts of gaining new information, using skills that we perform well, and yet spending time doing tasks that must be done. But all these variations confer a certain satisfaction since they are willingly undertaken and do not outrage human dignity.

These distinctions in the special educational treatment of handicapped children are important. Some of the so-called "play" that has been pressed upon handicapped children, always with the very best intentions, has been perilously near to drudgery (*slog*).

Figure 1-4 SOLITARY — A simple steering wheel becomes Dad's car. Note solitary doll play in background.

Solitary	Make-Believe
Apprenticeship	3P

Figure 1-5 PARALLEL — A classic example! (*Courtesy of L.D.S. Sixth Ward, Rexburg, Idaho*)

Figure 1-6 ASSOCIATE — Play in a sandbox in a courtyard type school playground. The children interact, enjoy and learn from each other.

Figure 1-7 COOPERATIVE — Animated conversation and descriptive gestures marked this incident of dramatic play. The children are taking definite roles. *(Courtesy of Omega Head Start, Phoenix, Arizona)*

Cooperative	Make-Believe
Research	4P

Figure 1-12   CONSTRUCTIVE — The end product of the play with pipes turned out to be a periscope.

- Make-believe play — the child uses toys, other materials, or even words to stand for something else that is not present. She wears Dad's shoes and she becomes Dad. She picks up a block and it becomes a heavy suitcase. This play begins during the child's second year, peaks during the fourth and early fifth years, then declines, although it is used in various forms throughout life. Simple make-believe play is easy to understand; let's describe some of the complex kinds of make-believe play:

  — Dramatic play — Although there are detailed sequences of symbolic levels of play (Nicolich 1977), for the purposes of this book, we can accept dramatic play as *pretend* play. (The more advanced student will want to study this in further detail.)

  — Fantasy play — (Often called *sociodramatic* play) is make-believe that involves interactions with others. This is a more complex type of play because the child must have greater knowlege about the world before he/she can work and develop that knowledge through play.

  — Superhero play — Many feel this is a type of fantasy play, but it is seen quite frequently in centers, schools, and homes. There is disagreement about how to

Figure 1-13   MAKE-BELIEVE — Complex fantasy of super-heroine play evolves as she becomes a famous singer or a model on TV. (*Courtesy of Omega Head Start, Phoenix, Arizona*)

handle this play. Many think it is a natural outlet for the children's feelings and need for control; others feel that it can get out-of-hand and stifles other types of creative playing.

A two-, almost three-year-old sees presents on a shelf that were left there by a visiting grandmother to be opened at his birthday party. He names the three presents "the dog, the cat, and the frog." He waves to them and talks to them. At the child's third birthday celebration he opens the presents with no qualms or reference to his former pretending. But now he takes the toy telephone (one of the birthday gifts) and starts having conversations with the absent grandmother.

As the third year passes, the three-year-old girl starts to have more complicated play with her dolls. She will pretend to drink out of the play bottle to see if it is just right, then feed her doll from the bottle. Most of her pretense play is development of a single scheme that extends her own actions.

As he shows through his spontaneous play that he is learning about living, concentration and the beginning of goal accomplishment is seen. A family has a cabin in the woods. A great many rocks have been placed so that people can walk over a marshy area to get to a higher rock area on the other side. (This might sound dangerous to some, but it is not, and supervising adult family members are there to watch the child's every move.) Sometime during the child's third year, he will announce that he can cross the rocks himself. As the adults hold their breath, he walks and jumps from rock to rock. No professional mountaineer guide has ever planned moves more carefully; the child's concentration is evident. When he reaches the other side the child will screech, "...and I didn't fall!" or "I made it, I made it!" Within a few moments after reaching his goal, the triumphant child changes into symbolic play, assuming a role. It may be his most recently watched super-hero from television/video viewing or he may proclaim that he's "boss of the rocks!" or some similar exclamation. His self-esteem soars because he realizes he has accomplished something he set out to do himself.

The four-year-old child usually has a sense of sex constancy by now (i.e., she knows that she is a girl and will always be a girl as she grows). But that fact has no bearing on her role-playing. She will announce that she will be "king" and a few minutes later that the king has turned into the grandest lion in the jungle. (How great it is if children of this age can play outside and be LOUD!) It is even better if the child can go on with her play and not have to stop "JUSTplaying" so he can go into the center and do a workbook drill sheet.

Much complex play during these years will have a realistic base, too. Sociodramatic play in which children act out roles of people in the environment about them becomes more frequent. Also, children will sometimes handle stressful situations with complex make-believe play. After a disaster such as a major flood, children will be seen enacting rescue operations and clean-up work. After such a disaster in my town a few years ago, I co-directed a temporary care center where parents could leave their children while they cleaned up the mess (aided by the wonderful volunteers). Although I had given lectures for years on dramatic play, I was amazed at the complexity of the children's role-taking and role-switching. Weeks later, children could be observed playing "flood" near their homes. Special play sessions were later held for some of the children whose homes were badly affected. "Flood play" continued for months. The children and their parents were surveyed when the reconstruction period was completed. None of the children seemed to have lasting scars from the trauma. The caregivers and parents believe play helped!

Dr. Sheridan felt that knowing about make-believe play was very important to professional workers, particularly those concerned with the health of the child. She noted that the child uses his play experiences to find probable causes and effects. He relates to activities that are observed and copied and deliberately invents increasingly complex make-believe situations for himself. In this way he practices and enjoys his acquired insights and skills. He also offers his comments upon the passing scene, improves his general knowledge and, most importantly of all, *refines his social communication*. Make-believe play depended upon a child's ability to receive and express his ideas in some form of language-code. Consequently its spontaneous employment is of considerable diagnostic significance to professional workers concerned with the health, welfare, and education of young children.

- Games-with-rules — the child and associates develop their own rules. There is tacitly acknowledged leadership that guides the others to improvise rules for cooperative play. Later, more formal games with already established rules are played. A full understanding and acceptance of the abstractions involved in sharing, taking turns, fair play, and accurate recording of results is presupposed. Team games (such as soccer) and games that can be played alone or in groups (such as foursquare)

Figure 1-14   GAMES-WITH-RULES — Almost six years old. When he learns the rules of the road he can ride on sidewalks, then streets. *(Courtesy of Dr. Ralph McBride, Rexburg, Idaho)*

become important. This play (Figure 1-14) begins in the third and fourth years and is widely used in the fifth and sixth years. The movement into games with established rules develops in the sixth or seventh year.

Piaget believed that there was a difference between imitation and play. Others view imitative play as a separate category of play. We will consider it later.

To review, the types of play I shall use are:

- Practice/exercise
- Constructive
- Make-believe, simple
- Make-believe, complex
- Games-with-Rules

Elements of Play

In childhood it is characteristic for the developing mind to be alert and curious and the body to be continually but purposefully active. These facts together with the characteristics of temperament the child displayed very early in life reveal the developing personality. When a child can be described as being emotionally healthy, useful, and

Figure 1-15   RESEARCH — "Hey, doesn't this fit in there?" observes Prentes as the children play with the math toys. *(Courtesy of Omega Head Start, Phoenix, Arizona)*

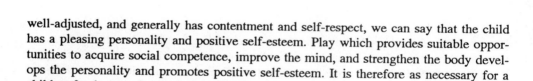

well-adjusted, and generally has contentment and self-respect, we can say that the child has a pleasing personality and positive self-esteem. Play which provides suitable opportunities to acquire social competence, improve the mind, and strengthen the body develops the personality and promotes positive self-esteem. It is therefore as necessary for a child as food, warmth, and protective care.

Many writers have listed the elements of play and what their functions are. My work with children has shown that the elements (functions) of play, represent for the child (according to his/her changing needs, moods, and intentions) research, occupational therapy, apprenticeship-to-living, and recreation.

Research means observation, discovery, exploration, speculation, Figure 1-15. When children become mobile their play shows much research. In fact, the twelve- to eighteen-month-old child is often called "The Little Scientist." As the child progresses, there are activities that we call *mastery play.* He learns to deal with his environment in a playful way. This type of mastery play would be explorative. Toys that are commonly called educational or learning-type often lead to research play. However, it is important to realize that all kinds of play media have the potential to be educational.

Occupational therapy provides relief from boredom, pain, or stress. Much spontaneous play is noted in this element of play. Rough-and-tumble play would sometimes be included under this category. The children (usually boys) are often relieving boredom or even stress. This is play-fighting, not real fighting. Expressions and even laughter give the clue to the therepeutic value of the play.

Figure 1-16 OCCUPATIONAL THERAPY — "The mama on the bus goes Sh! Sh! Sh!" sings the mama after the children said "Let's sing while we wait for the parade." Singing play relieved the boredom.

I observed a seven-year-old boy who loves baseball but was bored with watching his father's baseball game. Pres found three bottle caps. It was fascinating to watch the play that emerged. Pres's play eventually emerged into a clever game-with-rules. It relieved his boredom. In Figure 1-16 a mother and her children are waiting for a parade. The three-year-old is BORED! The mama started singing. Soon most of the children in the immediate area were singing and doing the actions and even making up verses to fit the situation of waiting for the parade. SPONTANEOUS! (Note: This therapeutic function of play is a topic of current interest and research both as it pertains to children and adults. I urge the student of this book to look for spontaneous therapeutic play that arises in naturalistic settings. There is much insight that can be gained from observing such play — especially in the ways that individuals handle the stresses of life.)

Apprenticeship-to-living concerns continuity of practice leading to competence in everyday skills, Figure 1-17. Imitative play would be included under this element of play; so would certain kinds of mastery play. Activities in the "rooms at home" area of a center and play with domestic objects are two examples that are easy to recall. Yet as one observes play there are many spontaneous acts that emphasize this element of play.

Recreation is simple, enjoyable FUN (Figure 1-18)! This does not need to be justified. Just notice the billion dollar industries that provide fun and recreation for adults. In fact, I propose that adults who care for children learn to appreciate this element of child-play — it is free and can be "simple, enjoyable fun" for the caregiver.

Figure 1-17 APPRENTICESHIP-TO-LIVING — He's gaining competency in basic life skills, but it's such FUN to mix the juice. (Maybe it's "ploy.")

Figure 1-18 RECREATION — Teacher's laugh and lap, a bunny to pet — genuine fun.

To review, the elements of play I will use are:

- Research
- Occupational Therapy
- Apprenticeship-to-Living
- Recreation

Note that the first letters of these elements of play form the the word *"ROAR."* (Another mnemonic device.) The child "roars with approval" when he/she is allowed to play — particularly when the play is spontaneous play. One sees children laughing and building good self-identity when play is occurring. Almost never does one see a child laughing while he/she is doing a worksheet drill page; seldom do these build good self-identity either.

Provisions for Play

Four provisions are of primary importance — playthings, playspace, playtime, and play-mates.

PLAYTHINGS must be appropriate for the child's age and stage of growth and development, Figure 1-19. They must not be too few or the child will lack stimulation, and not too many or he/she will become confused and unable to concentrate. Many toys that are available today are well-built and excellent for the child's play. Unfortunately, many are not and the caring adult must make discriminations when selecting toys for the child. The caregiver must not overlook playthings in nature or household items that the child loves

Figure 1-19 PLAYTHINGS — Teacher adds a board which becomes a ramp when tipped. A new plaything! Beginning science "play."

Figure 1-20   PLAYSPACE — She swings safely during a visit to a well-constructed playground. This playspace is an environment for all kinds of play.

to play with. In appendix B there is a list of all the toys mentioned in this text and shown in the illustrations. There are also suggestions for using this listing; these suggestions will help the reader learn more about playthings.

PLAYSPACE is needed for the freeranging activities, which are commonly shared with others, but every child must also possess a small personal territory which he knows is his own and which therefore provides a secure base. (This is as essential in centers as it is at home.) More attention is now being paid to outdoor playspaces, Figure 1-20. The stereotyped playgrounds with the same type of equipment are being replaced by playgrounds that incorporate nature and/or equipment that was designed by those who understand children's development.

PLAYTIME must be reasonably peaceful and predictable the majority of the time. It should be adequate for fulfillment of whatever activity is presently engaging the child's interest. Premature interruptions are likely to cause frustration. On the other hand, undue prolongation of a play period can lead to fading of purpose from boredom, loneliness, or feelings of neglect. These, of course, should be avoided if possible.

Television/video viewing must be considered when discussing time for play. Ninety-seven percent of the homes in the United States have television sets; in many homes, the television is on if anyone is there. This book will not be entirely anti-television — that would not be realistic for most families and in rare situations, some centers; but it will highly recommend that television/video watching be held to a minimum and carefully

Figure 1-21   PLAYTIME — Seven-year-old plays with her collection of stuffed toys. It's great that she has the time to play after a long day of school work.

monitored by caring adults. As those who guide young children learn more about the value of play and its potential for helping the child learn about living, perhaps we can convince others that children are entitled to time for play, especially spontaneous play, Figure 1-21. Therefore, the TV might often be turned off!

PLAYMATES are required at all stages of development, Figure 1-22. Encouraging adults are not only essential to dependent infants but also in the period of solitary play that is characteristic of children under two-and-one-half years. The adult playmate, usually the parent, older sibling, or caregiver can help this youngest child who is still unaware of such abstract principles as equal rights, sharing, and taking turns. Need for peer relationships increases as the child gets older. By four years of age most children are usually well able to hold their own in every sense of the word. In still later childhood, spontaneous peer-group play becomes progressively more elaborate and (a point of considerable significance) more strictly disciplined according to agreed regulations, observance of which provides most of the enjoyable element. Between seven and twelve, leisure-time activities become more selectively sex-determined. Outdoor games, particularly role-playing activities, tend to be played in exclusive masculine groups and feminine pairs or small groups. Male and female adolescents rediscover mutual common interests and gravitate into mixed groups again. The leisure-time occupations of adults include all sorts of sports, hobbies, arts, crafts, even further education and good works. It is noteworthy that individual tastes and particularly artistic gifts become obvious very early in life. They are often clearly apparent by seven or eight years of age.

Figure 1-22   PLAYMATES — Twins! Great friends! They can even rock together in the rocking chair. *(Courtesy of Joe Hamilton State Preschool, Crescent City, California)*

To review the "Provisions" for play:

- Playthings
- Playspace
- Playtime
- Playmates

BOOKS — "Read Me This Story" to "I Can Read It Myself"

Where do books fit into this framework of play that teaches children to learn about living? Everywhere!

Strictly speaking, books do not fit my definition of play because during many of the first years, the adult needs to read to the child. Therefore the child can not control the action. However, book-reading leads to great spontaneous play — play in every category! Also the wise adult (the companionate player) can often let the child take the lead, especially since most children want a favorite book read to them again and again. The adult can convey a genuine love of books and reading. This parent, teacher, or caregiver can listen to the child's questions and comments and respond appropriately. This stimulates effective language development. Often questions about a book can be answered by quickly setting up a play situation. (Example: The book is about dinosaurs. Materials can be found to set up a "time of the dinosaurs" play area. Dinosaurs can be drawn and taped to sticks and moved around the play space.) The possibilities are endless. When the child expresses enthusiastic interest in the story, a prop or two or a quick rearranging of the environment will often lead to dramatic play or fantasy play that is very creative. (Example: Acting out *CAPS FOR SALE* by Esphyr Slobodkina. An available sturdy bench can be the tree where the monkeys call "Tsk, Tsk, Tsk." Paper cups can be the caps, or children can pretend to have caps.) This builds great oral language skills, and proficiency in oral language is one of the best predictors of success in formal reading.

When illustrator Jenny Moser and I were developing the Framework of Play, she said, "You can put anything in the trunk of the vehicle." I responded, "I'll put language development in there because I think it is one of the most important reasons for determining that each child has time for spontaneous play. I'll include books, too, both when the child is reading and when the child is being read-to. It's an important part of the vehicle of learning through play."

THE "SPONTANEOUS WORK" OF YOUNG CHILDREN

For many years, the maxim "Play is the child's work" was used by most teacher trainers in early childhood education, including your author. No matter how strongly early childhood practitioners believed this, the general public still viewed the child's natural activities as "JUSTplay." Therefore, the maxim was generally dropped and a surge of information based on solid, empirical research on play appeared in all books and media interested in young children. This information stressed that play is valuable in and of itself; it does not have to parade as "work." However, as David Elkind, then president of the National Association for the Education of Young Children stated in his July 1988 editorial in *YOUNG CHILDREN* magazine: "I now believe that our labeling children's play as work was a mistake. Increasingly, I find myself explaining to media people, to elementary and secondary educators, and to parents that young children do work and that they are not always playing. The focus upon children's play as "work" or learning experience has taken attention away from the real work that children do and has suggested that all they do is play even if we stubbornly insist upon calling it "work."

Dr. Elkind continues: "Children learn *both* through accommodation and through assimilation. Both types of learning are important and complement one another....We have trouble making this point, in part at least, because we are accustomed to identifying learning with accommodation or work and to identifying recreation and fun with assimilation or play....I think we need to be more specific about what children learn from play. Perhaps when parents and educators of older children begin to understand how much learning young children are engaged in, whether in the form of work or play, we can get those in power positions to back off from the rigid curricula now being imposed at ever younger age levels."

"You said it well, David Elkind" I exclaimed aloud to the office walls when I read that editorial! Let us call children's efforts "work" or "play" or "work/play." Perhaps to those of us on the firing line it may be a matter of semantics. This is not a statement that diminishes in any way the excellent work of researchers, how they think, and the development of taxonomies. The important thing is that children are allowed their spontaneous play/work experiences. These experiences are the ones from which the children gain the most learning that will be used in LIFE!

PLAY AND DEVELOPMENTALLY APPROPRIATE PRACTICE

In order of appearance and quality of performance, a child's playtime accomplishments closely reflect his normal developmental progress. Every step forward depends upon achievement and consolidation of previous gains in development. Although their beginnings are readily distinguishable, the main types of play/work soon become inseparably integrated. They fall naturally into two groups: those mainly concerned with bodily skills and those concerned with human communications.

SAFETY

Each person who is involved with young children in any capacity has a responsibility to ensure the safety of the child. SAFETY CANNOT BE LEFT TO THE OTHER PERSON. Often, in a center, one person is designated as the main person responsible for the safety of the play environments. But it is each person's duty to constantly be aware of all elements of the environment where a child or children are playing or working. Playthings for young children must be safe to suck, handle, and drop; impossible to swallow, washable, and as unbreakable as possible. Playspaces must be free from hazards and as comfortable as possible. Outdoor playgrounds must be constantly surveyed to see that there are no dangerous places for the children. After all, our children are the nations's best resource. Each and everyone is precious!

APPLICATION FOR ADULTS

Apply the Framework of Play chart to the illustrations in the book or to pictures of play that you have taken. For example, in Figure 1-13, two children are playing in the housekeeping corner. The social dimension is cooperative because both are taking roles and interacting in that role. The type of play is make-believe as the children are using props in a representational way — perhaps even a super-heroine type of play is taking place. The element of play for the dressed-up child could be research as she speculates how a famous singer or model would act in a beautiful dress. The provisions for play are playspace, playtime, playthings, and a playmate. Another example is Figure 1-14. The almost six-year-old who rides on a bicycle path. How would this fit into the Framework of Play chart? It's evident that in social dimension the play is solitary. The type of play is probably complex make-believe play as the child pretends to be a competing cyclist or an older child in the apartment building. A game-with-rules may be involved as he follows bicycling regulations. The element of play illustrated could be apprenticeship-to-living (a good portion of the world's citizens ride a bike to work), but it is probably recreation — FUN! The provisions for play include playspace, playtime, and a plaything (the bike). No one can tell exactly what the framework of play is for that particular child at that mo-

ment, because no one can tell the thoughts on her mind. But this exercise is a point of reference for studying play. Almost everyone remembers learning to ride a bike. Marking the configuration helps the committed student to understand play, and therefore children, better.

Below each caption is a configuration with four spaces that represent the four wheels on the Vehicle of Play. Some of the configurations underneath the captions are filled out as examples. The student is urged to fill out the remainder including those beneath the captions of the photos in this section. For Figure 1-14, for example, the configuration would be:

Solitary	Make-Believe or Games-w-Rules
App.-to-Living or Recreation	3P

Note: "3 P" means that the picture shows three of the provisions for play — playspace, playtime, and playthings (stuffed animals). If there had been children riding bikes the configuration would say "4P" — indicating that playspace, playtime, playthings (bikes), and a playmate are shown.

OBSERVING

Figure 1-23 is an observation form based on the Framework of Play vehicle. Doing observations using this form is probably better than most other activities to learn about play. Of course, teaching/guiding the child is necessary for an in-depth understanding of the child. But a parent's/teacher's mind is on objectives, safety, the next part of the program, or home responsibility, etc. When one takes time to observe, the focus can be on a child (or children) and PLAY. As stated before, I have taught early education in some form for many years, but I learned about the great possibilities of a child learning about living through play as I have observed intently in naturalistic settings using this and similar observation forms.

Situations are so varied that I will say little about the places for observing, but I hope they will be as naturalistic as possible. (In a home setting, it is best to get someone else to "tend" the child so you can concentrate on observing. However, if this is not possible, notes can be jotted down as you work. After all, that is how Dr. Sheridan gained most of her knowledge about children.)

As you begin to observe, have the "Framework of Play Definition Page" available for reference, Figure 1-24. By this time, you will have studied these definitions of the categories in each of the four wheels of the Vehicle of Play, but the reference page will help in your observing. After a first observing session, you will probably find that you will need to study the definitions in the four wheels again. Understanding comes as you do this, however. You will learn more about the ages and stages of children in their development of play in the next section and you will find that your ability to gain understanding and knowledge of children will increase. I find it an exciting way to learn. I'm certain you will too.

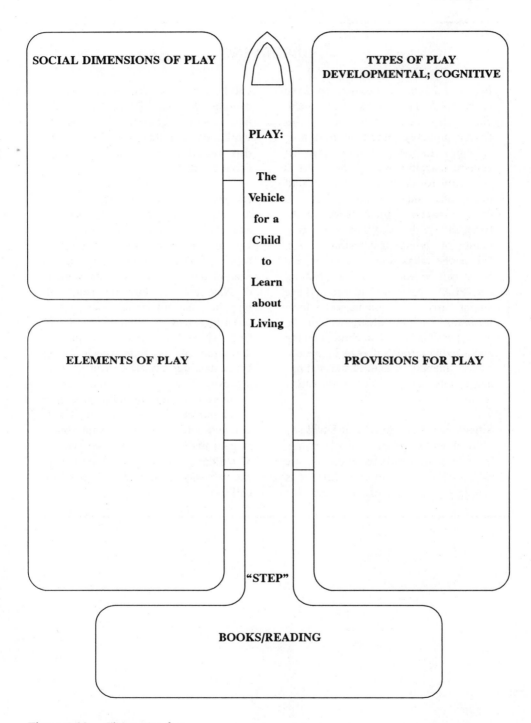

Figure 1-23   Observation form

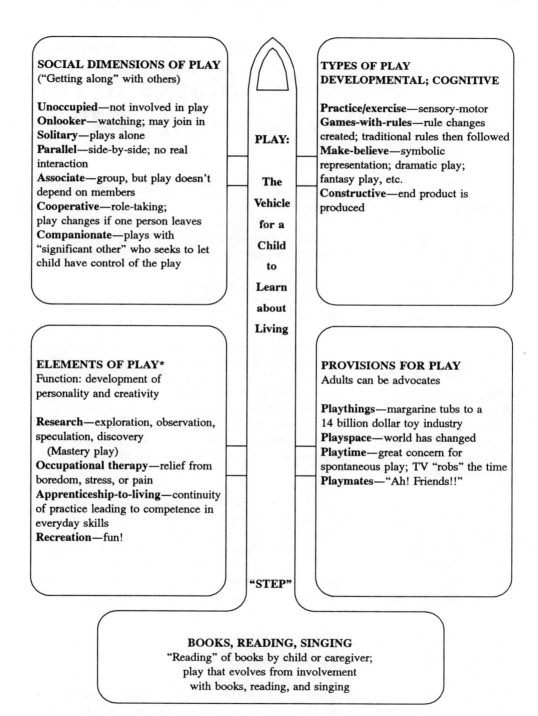

SOCIAL DIMENSIONS OF PLAY
("Getting along" with others)

Unoccupied—not involved in play
Onlooker—watching; may join in
Solitary—plays alone
Parallel—side-by-side; no real
interaction
Associate—group, but play doesn't
depend on members
Cooperative—role-taking;
play changes if one person leaves
Companionate—plays with
"significant other" who seeks to let
child have control of the play

PLAY:

The

Vehicle

for a

Child

to

Learn

about

Living

**TYPES OF PLAY
DEVELOPMENTAL; COGNITIVE**

Practice/exercise—sensory-motor
Games-with-rules—rule changes
created; traditional rules then followed
Make-believe—symbolic
representation; dramatic play;
fantasy play, etc.
Constructive—end product is
produced

ELEMENTS OF PLAY*
Function: development of
personality and creativity

Research—exploration, observation,
speculation, discovery
  (Mastery play)
Occupational therapy—relief from
boredom, stress, or pain
Apprenticeship-to-living—continuity
of practice leading to competence in
everyday skills
Recreation—fun!

PROVISIONS FOR PLAY
Adults can be advocates

Playthings—margarine tubs to a
14 billion dollar toy industry
Playspace—world has changed
Playtime—great concern for
spontaneous play; TV "robs" the time
Playmates—"Ah! Friends!!"

"STEP"

BOOKS, READING, SINGING
"Reading" of books by child or caregiver;
play that evolves from involvement
with books, reading, and singing

Figure 1-24   Framework of Play; definition page

Ages and Stages in the Development of Play

THOUGHT QUESTIONS

- What are the advantages of knowing the various stages of a child's play?
- How can the "Vehicle of Play Framework" be applied to each play incident recorded in pictures or video frames?
- What is the adult's role as the child engages in spontaneous play?
- How can the adult help the child advance to the next level of play if that appears to be developmentally appropriate?

Davey's mother walked into the kitchen to find her two-year-old son on a chair in front of the open junk drawer systematically throwing things one at a time on the floor. "Davey," cried Mom, "what are you doing?" He looked up with a grin and said, "I'se sinding things out more!" ("I'm finding out more about things!") This reply tells much about the normal development of young children — they are busy discovering how the world around them operates. Play is a vehicle that helps the child. From his infancy when he playfully shakes his rattle until the primary grades of school when he and his friends make up rules to guide their spontaneously created games, the child is involved in different stages of play.

In order to interpret the play of young children (particularly of exceptional children) and make suitable provisions for their needs, it is appropriate to consider the ages and stages of development at which various significant evidences of behavior usually appear. It is important to bear in mind that wide individual differences are to be expected, and that for the sake of brevity, numerous intermediate phases and transitions are necessarily omitted here. As stated before, actual ages at time of photography are recorded underneath the photographs. They are not necessarily the earliest age at which the indicated play appears.

THE SENSORIMOTOR PERIOD: FROM BIRTH TO TWO YEARS

The work of Jean Piaget helps us learn about the child's normal development of play as well as her cognitive development. The age span from birth to two years of age is called the *sensorimotor period* because the child learns through her senses as well as her movements. There are six stages within this period.

Figure 2-1   Seven weeks — The baby smiles and looks toward the light, but "true play" does not begin yet.

The Newborn

Using the first stage, from birth to one month, practice and repetition of reflexes are noted. The newborn baby does not need to be taught to move her limbs, to suck, or to cry, and she quickly learns to attract and welcome her caregivers' attentions. Full-term babies usually gaze steadily at their mothers or caregivers; premature babies often do not. Now, these early arrivals are given special stimulation in neonatal care nurseries or at home. However, the full-term babies are able to do much more than people formerly thought they could do. Although they are awake for relatively short periods of the day, they begin interactions with their first playmates — usually the mother and more and more often, the father — soon after they are born.

One to Four Months

Although the young infant's vigorous movements and smiles, Figure 2-1, and cooing when handled and talked to obviously indicate responses to enjoyable stimulation, Figure 2-2, what is commonly regarded as "true" play does not begin yet. This "play" which usually starts in the form of purposefully-directed reaching for toys, becomes possible only with the disappearance of certain primitive reflexes unnecessary to describe here. Then play is no longer merely evidence of stimulus and predictable response but increasingly a question of selective sensory intake (reception) which is then processed within the brain (interpretation) and results in some appropriate motor outcome (expression). The two-month-old can usually lift his head just enough to turn from side to side. However, by ten to twelve weeks of age, the child lying on his back, head in mid-line, deliberately brings his hands together over his upper chest and, converging his eyes upon them, engages in active, interlacing fingerplay. About the same time, when lying on his stomach, holding his head and shoulders up steadily, he will open and shut his hands, scratching at the surface on which he lies, obviously with some appreciation of the simultaneous production of sight and sound, Figure 2-3. Given a holdable toy (such as a rattle or

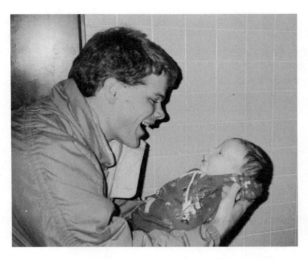

Figure 2-2   Two months — The infant's cooing when handled indicates his response to enjoyable stimulation.

Companionate	Pr./Ex.
App. to Living	3P

wooden spoon) he clasps it firmly and brings it towards his face, sometimes bashing his chin, but usually any glances he makes at it are fleeting. He finds it difficult to control his head, neck, and eye muscles and keep his hand in "static" grasp at the same time. By about fourteen weeks, however, he can hold the toy and steadily regard it.

Figure 2-3   Three months — Lying on her front, lifting her head and resting on her forearms, she scratches at the table cover enjoying the simultaneous sight and sound of her finger movements. *(Courtesy of Pugmire Photography)*

Solitary	Pr./Ex.
Research	3P

Piagetians often refer to first acquired adaptations. This is because the infant begins to repeat reflexes and random actions for pleasure. He runs his tongue around his lips and he feels a pleasant sensation. Wow! He does that again! He will also kick his legs over and over again. His pleasure is evident! The infant also recognizes that an object is a separate entity. However, if he drops the rattle he is holding, he makes no move to pick it up; it ceases to exist for him.

Four to Eight Months

At about eighteen to twenty weeks, the baby can reach for and grasp an offered rattle, look at it with prolonged gaze, and shake it. She can also take it to her mouth and then withdraw it. She can hold it between her two hands, clasping and unclasping it alternately. She can drop it by opening both hands wide, but cannot yet place it down neatly and deliberately. As is evident, these actions are a big advancement for the baby, and adults seldom appreciate this progress — often because we do not realize the scope of the development taking place.

By six months her general neuromuscular control, manipulation, ability to see objects in dimensions, and hand-eye coordination are so advanced that she can reach out for and seize hold of any play object within the reach of her extended arms. She has discovered the possession of feet and often uses them as auxiliary claspers, Figure 2-4. She brings every grasped object to her mouth. She is still incapable of voluntary hand release. She recognizes meaningful objects when they recur in familiar circumstances.

Figure 2-4   Four-and-a-half months — Having discovered her possession of feet, she reaches out in foot-mouth coordination. *(Courtesy of Dr. Veryl Larsen)*

Figure 2-5 Six months — Who is imitating whom? Companionate play between mom and baby sister while brother is in the toddler playschool.

She clearly demonstrates the ability to differentiate between familiar people and unfamiliar strangers from about six to seven months. Each semester we have parents of our toddler and preschool children who watch their child from one of our observation booths. I find that some of the most interesting observing is often the companionate play of the mother or father and their six- to seven-month-old baby (the sibling of the preschool or toddler child). The joy of the baby as he/she plays with that familiar caregiver is often imitative and is accompanied by laughs and smiles, Figure 2-5.

At about seven months she begins to appreciate the functional "twoness" of hands and a week or two later, of feet, Figure 2-6. She can hold two objects, one in each hand simultaneously using firm palmar grasp and bring her hands together to "match" them. She can now pass a toy from one hand to the other with voluntary hand release.

This third substage of Piaget's sensorimotor stage is often referred to as procedures for making interesting sights last. Piaget recorded an example of this type of action done by his own daughter, Lucienne. She accidentally kicked some cloth dolls hanging from the hood of her bassinet. She smiled and repeated the action. Piaget called the movements "concomitants of joy." However, in the next few days Lucienne repeated the action without smiling and with an interest that was "intense and sustained." She seemed to study the phenomenon. It was only after many days when Lucienne found repeated success in her actions, that she smiled again (Piaget, 1952, pp.157–158). Lucienne was

Figure 2-6   Eight-and-a-half months — Creeping toward an eye-catching toy and reaching for it. (Note the appearance of her lips.)

interested in objects outside her own body; she studied the response of the hanging dolls when she kicked them and found ways to make them move again by actions of her body.[*]

The infant is beginning to comprehend the permanence of *people* but not yet the permanence of *things*. When a toy falls from her hand, unless it is within her continuing range of vision, it ceases to exist for her.

Eight to Twelve Months

From about eight months the child sits steadily on the floor, stretches out in all directions for toys within his arm's reach without falling over. He begins to creep and reach towards eye-catching objects, Figure 2-7. He begins to throw toys about for the satisfaction not only of motor achievement, but for the interest of seeing and hearing the sequence of events that occur when objects fall, roll away, and come to a standstill. He enjoys producing the simultaneous noise and tactile sensation of banging or sliding about solid objects such as blocks, bells, or small domestic items on hard flat surfaces.

---

[*]   *Lucienne was actually in her third month when Piaget recorded this incident, but it is often used in literature to illustrate the third stage, "making interesting sights last." The author has found that it is an example students remember as they observe. It also shows that the stated ages of any of the stages are only approximate.*

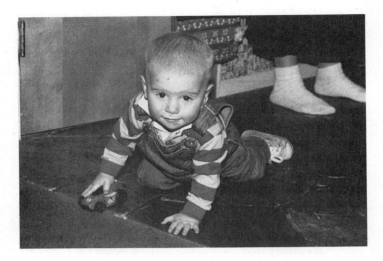

Figure 2-7   Ten months — He adds a throaty "car sound" to his play. He seeks to have his mom/caregiver close by for reassurance or cooperation in play.

Companionate	Pr./Ex.
Research	3P

At about nine months he usually begins to have a more complex playing with his toys. Two wooden spoons can be banged together or a spoon can be rattled in a container. A cup will be brought to the mouth. A bell with a handle will be hit on the table to make a noise. Sheridan pointed out that at this stage girls tended to be a little more advanced than boys, but boys might already show more vigorous locomotor activity. At twelve months girls also tend to engage in "give and take" play with caregivers, but boys usually do this somewhat later, although boys often show more interest than girls in simple ball games, rolling and throwing from a sitting position.

All babies, as they become more mobile, increasingly seek proximity to their mothers or familiar caregivers. This is partly for the reassurance of his/her constant availability and partly to seek cooperation in play. The old game of "peek-a-boo!" is brand new to the baby of this age. But now the parent/caregiver is so necessary to the baby that he is distressed if that person leaves the room outside of range of sight and hearing. Many a mother has wondered when her child is this age if she'll ever be able to use the bathroom in peace and privacy again!

Piagetians often talked about the infant coordination of means and ends during this stage. At about nine to ten months the child becomes aware of the permanence of objects. He will lift a cushion to look underneath it for a plaything which, while he watches, first has been half-hidden (i.e., with a part of it showing) and two or three weeks later, wholly covered. He leans over the side of his stroller to keep a falling plaything in view. He has a better idea of the use of objects and will now grasp a bell and hit it on a surface to make a sound; by ten months he will seize the top of the handle with one hand and ring it. This is the stage where he loves to play the game "disappear and reappear." Endless versions of games are played such as putting a small ball under one's hand saying "Where did it go?" to the delighted child who moves the hand to reveal the ball. He also begins to anticipate what objects mean. Sometimes Dad and Mom are amazed when their previously complying baby scoots away from them at the mere sight of his nighttime pajamas.

From nine to twelve months, the child has clearly begun to understand the import of his parents'/caregiver's spoken communications. First, he shows awareness of the cadences of vocal intonation and then of a few single word-forms. Eventually he understands simply phrased instructions and prohibitions that are addressed to him personally in recurring situations. He is beginning to find meaning in his familiar world. He likes to watch and listen to his familiar adults as they go about their daily occupations and periodically to be touched, talked to, and played with as they pass. He uses gestures such as pointing to communicate.

The baby's attentions, relationships, and play are still engaged and satisfied mainly at the level of on-going perceptions; but his immediate, brief imitations indicate that he has come into possession of a short-term memory and is proceeding with the establishment of a long-term memory bank. For the latter, he will gradually pile up all sorts of memoranda related to significant physical, cognitive, and affective experiences, for the purpose of instantaneous recognition, retrieval, and creative assembly when he needs them.

Dr. Sheridan believed that early play, because of its reliance on precepts rather than concepts, may remain endlessly repetitive unless the mother (caregiver) indicates the next step. This is usually done instinctively, but not always. A non-participating mother/caregiver therefore needs help to understand his/her own essential part in the furtherance of her child's optimum development. Most child advocates have known this, but only in this past decade have there been studies that have very effectively combined important theoretical and practical concerns. Jay Belsky, Mary Kay Goode and Robert Most from Pennsylvania State University have done this and shown that mothers who focused their infants' attention on objects had children who engaged in more competent play (Belsky et al, 1980, p. 1176), Figure 2-8.

Professional workers also need reminding that a mother in the ordinary home cannot just stop what she is doing in order to play with her child; but her encouragement towards his independent mobility and her frequent affectionate communications, however brief, are all-important in promoting his competence. In these often brief, but effective ways, a child learns during his first year that things keep their properties even in movement, but the behavior of people tends to be most interestingly, though not frighteningly, unpredictable. He must be able to move about this familiar world so as to acquire a working knowledge of its nature and its possibilities. He must also learn to acquire a measure of control over his own behavior and relationships within it, before he can communicate his wishes, attitudes, and intentions with regard to it.

Figure 2-8   Mom knows how to focus her baby's attention. Her child shows more competent play because of this.

At home or in family day-care, a child balances his need for close proximity to his parent or caregiver with his need to explore, nicely integrating motor activity with sensory alertness and emotional satisfaction, Figure 2-9. He also recognizes situational constancy in home surroundings. For instance, he knows that if his mother or caregiver is busy temporarily she will not suddenly disappear beyond his power to summon her back, as she might do, say, in the open park. He can therefore begin to tolerate extending intervals of time and space between them.

Again, professional workers and planners of care centers must realize that the infant for whom they have responsibility many hours of the day — and sometimes night — also deserves a stability of environment. He deserves adults who will give him "situational constancy."

Twelve to Eighteen Months

In this period a child becomes increasingly mobile, inquisitive and self-willed, and sometimes difficult to control. Her world of attention is rapidly expanding. She is no longer satisfied with her former lively acceptance of incidents she sees or hears. She loses interest in events that are presented mainly as distant, repetitious, unrewarding, visual displays and sound sequences. She needs to take a closer look at and a more active part in what is happening. This is shown by her obvious dawning recognition of cause and effect. This understanding is first seen in her prompt imitation of activities with which she has firsthand experience. It could be called an "action echolalia." An example would be that the child will accidentally pull her own hair and then pull it again purposely to

Figure 2-9   Eleven-and-a-half months — Holding on to furniture, he cruises about the room — investigating every object of interest enroute.

see if the hurt is repeated. Then she will go on to pulling other things — sometimes her mother/caregiver's hair!

From this stage she proceeds to demonstrate more obvious and prolonged "definition-by-use" in relation to common objects, such as drinking from an empty cup, or bringing a brush to her hair and then combing her caregiver's hair, Figure 2-10). At first, these activities are very brief, but soon they become more extended in scope and in time. They are sequentially correct and directed towards some purposeful activity; it appears that the toddler has an "aim in view."

This twelve to eighteen month old child is sometimes called "The Little Scientist." She is dominated by an urge to explore and exploit her environment. She is rapidly discovering the implication of container and contained, that is, she likes to dump, load it back up and dump again, Figure 2-11. She looks into boxes and cupboards to manipulate, smell, and taste the objects within, sometimes presenting them to her mother/caretaker, occasionally making some show of replacing them, but more often scattering them around the floor. She manipulates blocks with good pincer grasp, but seldom aligns more than two or three together on a flat surface or in a "tower," in imitation or spontaneously.

She still employs percussion tools to experiment to see if sound and strike go together. She tears paper to enjoy the simultaneous feel, sound, and sight of this activity. As the weeks go by, with increasing skill in upright movement, she pushes and pulls large-wheeled toys and guides small ones by hand or on the end of a string. She uses smaller-wheeled toys to transport collections of objects from one place to another, deliberately increasing the weight and complexity of her loads and the size of her stockpiles.

Figure 2-10   Fifteen months — She demonstrates "definition by use" by playing with a patient
adult.

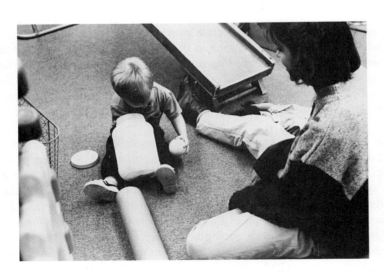

Figure 2-11   Sixteen months — "Dump and Fill" — a basic play activity of the toddler. Often,
it's more "dump" than "fill."

Companionate	Pr./Ex.
App. to Living	4P

She still throws her toys about, but less often and mainly as an expression of annoyance or to discard them if they cease to interest her. She usually has no concern for direction or place of fall. Her interests are still closely tied to everyday family and domestic realities. She begins to engage in short episodes of symbolic play, particularly role-playing. She greatly enjoys active use of ordinary or child-sized replicas of familiar objects like shopping carts, brushes, pails, cups and saucers, pots, pans, telephones, furniture, and garden tools.

At this developmental stage of limited cognitive, social, and language appreciation, a doll or animal toy is treated like any other plaything. Although she likes to carry one about with her everywhere, may name (i.e., verbally label) it correctly and strongly resist being parted from it because it is her personal belonging, as yet it holds no true emotional significance as a symbol of a loved, animate being.

Piagetians often refer to the one-year-old as the child who is experimenting in order to see, Figure 2-12. The information given above shows why. Knowing about this sub-stage will help the reader appreciate the age as a fascinating one.

Language acquisition is starting to flourish. Some children are talking in very simple sentences by eighteen months. More are saying between three to fifty words. Many of these are said as holophrases where one word means a whole sentence. "PLAY!" might mean, "Come over here and interact with me; I'm bored with my own company." These little ones understand a great deal more than their spoken language allows them to convey. Nonverbal gestures and actions can be observed as having meaning as the child plays. One can see why the term Active Play is sometimes used instead of "Practice/

Figure 2-12   Seventeen months — He "experiments in order to see." Here he experiments on a drum with a handle.

Exercise Play" because so much of what this little scientist is doing is related to actively finding out about the world.

Simple work can be done as long as the parent/caregiver is right beside the child and does not have unrealistic expectations. The child might put three or four blocks back in the proper container, but she will have to have much encouragement. On the other hand, if you watch her repeat a new skill like climbing a large, simple ride-it toy again and again, you realize that the effort could truly be called "work."

There are social implications that should be mentioned at this stage. Owing to immature preoccupation with the "me" and only very primitive realization of the "not me," this just-turned-toddler tends to treat live animals and other children with similar apparent lack of affection or protective concern. A young child quickly learns that living creatures usually do things to her with some intention, while objects do not. Consequently, so far as she is concerned, young babies who do not intend anything towards her are not yet living personalities in their own right. They are merely objects to be manipulated, pushed about, or rejected as the whim takes her. Behavior that sometimes appears to the adult onlooker to be due to "sibling jealousy" is much more likely due to lack of the concept of family relationships. At this age, relationships are not understood. Social learning is undoubtedly entirely ego-centrated at first, i.e., it is "self-tied" rather than "self-ish." This would explain why her early definition-by-use activities directly involve her everyday care, e.g., the use of feeding utensils, toilet articles, and items of clothing. Acceptable "detached-from-self" activities (that lead later to the practice of unselfishness, sharing, taking turns, and eventually to compassionate behavior) does not — indeed, cannot — develop until a child has first learned the primary distinction of "me" and "not me." Then the distinction of "me" and "you" and finally the distinction of "us" and "them," which is the keystone of social communication are acquired. At least some of this learning depends upon appreciation of what is "mine" and what is "not mine," what is "yours" and "theirs."

Until this final stage of cognitive and emotional maturation has been reached, the child's egocentricity leads her to the unshakable conviction that, as a matter of course, all things rightfully belong to her. Her philosophy might be stated as being: "I come, I see, I grab. What I have, I hold."

APPLICATION FOR CAREGIVERS

The lesson for caregivers is obvious. As soon as the child is mobile, she should be provided with some playthings and a place (or territory) that are indisputably her own, so that she may learn not only the satisfactions but the accepted conventions of personal and territorial possession including the need to respect the rights of others. One very fine day-care home has an accessible "open" cube for each child. I am amazed at the way each little one realizes that this space is "mine!" She might not spend much time there, but she knows it is a place to go where she can find *her* things.

Eighteen to Twenty-Four Months

Between eighteen and twenty-four months the child is able to:

- take advantage of improved control of his body and limbs, Figure 2-13
- engage in many gross motor activities such as pushing, pulling, and carrying of large objects, climbing in and out of boxes, climbing on low walls and steps, Figure 2-14
- show increased interest in the nature and detailed use of small objects such as those found in handbags, boxes, and other spaces in the home/center, Figure 2-15
- sit on a small sled and have enough independence to be pushed down a small, snowy incline alone

His explorations are endless and since his sense of danger, like his understanding and use of language, are still very limited, while his desire of independent action is boundless, he requires constant supervision to protect him from danger.

His newly found manipulative abilities allow him to rummage among the contents of anything available to him. He throws some objects away from him, pulls others to pieces, and tears off wrappers. He enjoys banging, hammering, poking. However, given three or four suitable, durable toys like building blocks, cars and trucks, wooden or plastic trains that link together, and sturdy miniature people that fit into holes in moveable playthings, he will play contentedly at floor level for prolonged periods. Sturdy dolls and teddy bears and a selection of simple educational toys will keep him engaged in solitary play provided that a familiar and attentive adult is near. He likes putting small toys in and out of containers. Once he has discovered or been given the idea, he builds towers of blocks

Figure 2-13 Nineteen months — He pulls the fire engine as he walks backwards and around the corner. He's proud of his accomplishment.

Figure 2-14   Twenty months — Like all children this age he has an irresistible urge to get in and out of large boxes, perhaps learning his own relative size and position.

Solitary	Pr./Ex. or M.B.
App. to Living	3P

Figure 2-15   Twenty-two months — Handbags provide endless opportunities for exploration, manipulation, imitation, and sometimes danger! Be aware!

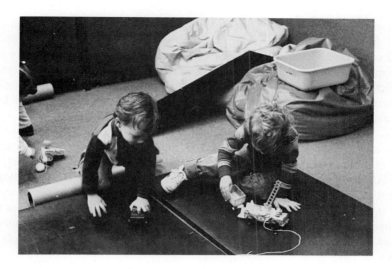

Figure 2-16   Twenty-four months — "inventions of new means through mental combinations." Notice that he has solved the linkage problem of the truck and trailer.

Parallel	Pr./Ex.
Research	4P

varying from three blocks at eighteen months to six or more at two years. He experiments for lengthening periods of time with elemental substances like water and sand, or moldable materials like clay and dough. He uses his hands and simple tools effectively; but as yet, he has little ability to plan or achieve an end product.

His drawings are still in the nature of widespread brushwork demanding good coordination of hand and eye but lacking pictorial representation. His manipulations of pencils and paintbrushes show increasingly competent use of the fingers and thumb. Although one hand is tending to show dominance, such preference is still quite variable and he continues to use either hand freely and sometimes both together. Definite right- or left-handedness is often not established until later.

Piagetians refer to this sixth substage as inventions of new means through mental combinations: the beginnings of thought. The children from eighteen to twenty-four months form mental representations of cause and effect independent of their immediate perceptions. The child shows by his correctly serialized imitations of familiar adult activities that he already possesses a useful stock of sensory and kinesic memoranda, although these still remain centered on himself as the hub of his universe, Figure 2-16.

In the early role and situational pretend play that is characteristic of this stage, he uses materials ready at hand, but in a fragmentary way. For instance, while playing for a few moments pretending to put himself to bed, he lies down, closes his eyes, and pulls a cover

over himself, but only if cushions or coverings are available. He goes through the move-ments of driving a car usually making suitable engine noises, if he has a seat and steering wheel of sorts. He pretends to read a book if there is one there. He puts two or three toys together meaningfully, a doll on a chair, or bricks in a truck, but seldom as yet making one object represent another or using mime to symbolize absent things or events. He needs literal play materials at this age. More abstract, free-form materials will be used as he gets older.

By eighteen months he usually speaks a few single words in appropriate context and a number of meaningful utterances (holophrases) such as "gimme" (give me), "der-tih" (there it is), or, in questioning cadence, "what-da?" (what is that?). His intonations greatly help intelligibility, but in order to be sure of what he is saying, it is necessary to know what he is actually doing. At about twenty-one months he begins to put two or more real words together to frame little sentences. These usually refer to very familiar matters or to needs and happenings in the here-and-now. He comprehends most of the simple language addressed to him.

Girls begin to treat their dolls and stuffed animals in caregiving fashion at about eighteen to twenty months, boys a little later. At about twenty-one months both begin to demon-strate their appreciation that miniature toys (i.e., dollhouse size) represent things and people in the real world. They clearly show this externalization (or expressions) of pre-viously internalized experiences by spontaneously arranging the little toys in meaningful groups, by actively indicating their use in everyday situations, and often by simulta-neously talking about them (another example of the beginning of thought). It is notewor-thy that from the outset girls show preference for play with domestic objects, and boys for miniature cars and other items of transport. This type of play, which extends rapidly after two years, proved of considerable help to Dr. Sheridan in her differential diagnosis of delays in the development of spoken language.

For some time however, although they correctly name and delicately manipulate these little toys, both boys and girls remain somewhat confused regarding the size of the toys in relation to themselves. They will try to sit on a miniature chair, to ride astride a miniature horse, or to step into a miniature vehicle. A little later, when they have realized these impossibilities for themselves, they may still attempt to place disproportionately large dolls or teddy bears in much smaller buggies or trucks.

From fifteen to eighteen months onwards a child also becomes increasingly interested in picture books, first to recognize and name people, animals, objects, and familiar actions (like eating or drinking, getting into a car, or mailing a letter). Soon he can follow a simple story read aloud to him while he looks at the pictures. Next he begins to make comments and ask questions. Some of this love of books and stories, which is very beneficial to his language development, is associated with his continued need for close proximity to his mother or other familiar caregivers of whom he remains strongly posses-sive, Figure 2-17. He is still incapable of such abstract concepts as sharing or taking turns.

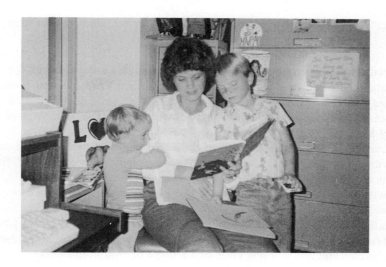

Figure 2-17   Two-year-old (with five-year-old) — Some of his love of books is his continued need for close proximity to his mother/caregiver of whom he remains possessive.

Companionate	
Recreation	4P

Books

Social implications of this age are that the child is a law unto himself, strongly resenting any infringement upon what he considers to be his constitutional rights which he defends with vigor and determination. He has yet to develop consideration for others, especially for age-peers and children younger and more helpless than himself. This is neither jealousy nor aggression in the adult sense. It is a normal phase of socialization. We do not expect a child to run before he can walk. Like all primary learning processes, the acquisition of ability to record things and events from another person's perspective necessitates a certain measure of neurological maturation, appropriate experience, and consistent understanding of his parents and other caregivers.

SPONTANEOUS PLAY FROM BIRTH TO TWO

Constant sympathetic, but non-stressful adult encouragement to engage in every sort of spontaneous play is essential not only to the contentment but to the fundamental learning of children between one and two years. From his use of playthings which he finally incorporates into make-believe play, a child first discovers through his visual, auditory, and tactile perceptions what they are and what special properties that they possess. Then he goes on to learn what he can do with them and finally how he can adapt them to his own requirements, constructional or make-believe.

To review "Play: A Vehicle to Learn about Living" for the sensorimotor stage (Birth to age two):

- Social: Play is mostly onlooker, solitary, and companionate; although there is some parallel and associative play. Brief incidents of cooperative play are seen.
- Types: Practice/exercise (sometimes called "Active" or "Functional") are the main types with a fair amount of constructive play observed. The beginnings of symbolic play are significant to the development of the child.
- Elements of Play: The research and the apprenticeship-to-living functions of play are important to this age level. The child is developing the concept of "fun" (Recreation).
- Provisions for Play: Important at any age level, these are the child's world during these years.
- Reading; Language: The foundations are laid. The child develops his first interest in books and a basic love for them. When he is being read to, he is also close to his parent/caregiver and this gives him a sense of trust in his world.

TWO-YEAR-OLDS

From the age of two years, a child becomes increasingly skillful in every form of *motor activity*. (The usual stages are summarized in a sequence of pictures in Section 3.) She lifts and carries, climbs, leaps, and runs. She can ride her tricycle forward, using the pedals, steer it around corners, and back it up, Figure 2-18. He kicks, throws and catches balls, albeit rather clumsily, but with ever-growing efficiency. He can walk down steps

Figure 2-18   Two years — She has backed her vehicle into this space. This demonstrates motor control and development of spatial sense.

APPLICATION FOR TEACHER/CAREGIVERS

At this point, the book *Developmentally Appropriate Practice* should be mentioned. This book is a policy statement by the National Association for the Education of Young Children. It gives guidelines for appropriate learning activities for the various ages. Of course, it strongly recommends play for all stages of early childhood, and gives strong, direct recommendations for these earliest years.

---

but it takes great concentration. (The usual stages are summarized in a sequence of pictures in Section 3.) He can walk down steps but it takes great concentration.

Her manipulations and constructive skills steadily improve. She builds a tower of eight to ten blocks. She holds a pencil, crayon, or felt tip pen halfway down the shaft or near the point, scribbling or imitating to and fro lines and circles on a sheet of paper. She also works with brushes or chalks on an easel covering large areas with color. She enjoys simple jigsaw puzzles and can match four or five colors and several shapes. These may include a few simple block-capital letters, but she usually cannot yet name or copy any of these. She should never be pressed to remember letters at this stage although occasionally a particularly interested child may draw one or two and is delighted to show off her accomplishments.

The two-year-old now appreciates many of the standard educational toys, such as the various puzzle-type toys where big pieces or objects are placed in appropriate holes or spaces. Nesting blocks or cups, screw toys, rings on sticks, "Duplo" or waffle blocks are popular. The house, school, service station, parking building, barn, and other miniature buildings with their miniature people and animals remain favorites and become used even more in both practice/exercise play and then in make-believe play as the child progresses. Two-year-olds, of course, use available materials from around the house such as hard plastic containers, and the traditional pots and pans. Early education centers that are tuned into the needs of their toddlers often have similar materials for their children to use.

Children of two instinctively use a lively form of "total communication" composed sometimes separately but more often simultaneously of words, gestures, and mime. These developments are immediately reflected in play. They still follow familiar adults around the house or center, imitating and joining in work routines. They like to push things back into place; then they call attention to their efforts and demand approval. They ask innumerable simple questions, especially as they approach three. Extending earlier role-playing, they invent little make-believe domestic situations such as sweeping floors, baby-caring, cooking, making beds, serving meals, taking care of pets, and delivering the mail. These activities become increasingly organized and prolonged and are "played out" with high seriousness. During these mini-dramas they often talk aloud to themselves in appropriate terms, describing and explaining what they are doing, instructing themselves with regard to their immediately forthcoming actions or formulating their uncertainties.

Figure 2-19   Two years — These children add relevant dialogue to their role playing. the big box with its "window" has stimulated pretense play. (*Courtesy of Ricks College, Toddler Lab*)

Cooperative	M.B.
App. to Living	4P

Later they extend their inventions, adding some relevant dialogue to their role-playing as mama or daddy, doctor, teacher, truck driver, or grocery checker. Often a big box with a "window" cut in it stimulates interesting spontaneous play, Figure 2-19.

They indicate the beginnings of forward planning, such as collecting suitable items for a teddy bear party or materials to drive a make-believe car.

The two-year-old's moveable "self-space" remains chiefly relative to herself and her caregivers, Figure 2-20. She is now prepared to admit one or two familiar children briefly into her play-world and to venture intermittently into theirs. Although they play in close proximity, the play itself is mainly solitary, so that each child needs her own set of playthings and her own bit of territory.

Since ability to communicate is limited and the need to share adult attentions and play-things is not yet sufficiently understood, relationships with age-peers are unstable and disputes are likely to be frequent. At this developmental stage, a child seems to realize her physical separateness before she appreciates her cognitive and affective individuality. For some time therefore, she remains convinced that her mother or principal caregiver automatically apprehends what she is feeling, needing, and intending. Apparently, however, under three years or so, she does not expect other children to share the inner workings of her mind but just assumes her own right to exercise her dictatorship. Hence, in her view, a desired toy only happens to be attached to another child. The living child who holds on to "her" toy is of little consequence.

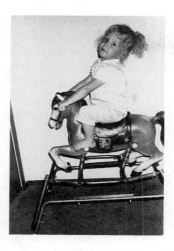

Figure 2-20   Two years — Girl on rocking horse, a toy loved by many children. Her self-space is chiefly for herself and her carergivers.

Age two is the beginning of the preoperational stage of cognitive development according to Piagetian theorists. It is fascinating to observe them as they get into more and more incidents of symbolic play, Figure 2-21. A two-year-old child delighted in taking a toilet paper tube and holding it by the side of her face as a telephone receiver. She practiced

Figure 2-21   Two-and-a-half years — A decorated hat in a "hands on" museum becomes a symbolic prop.

her language skills as she called grandmas, grandpas, daddy at work, etc. Her mother, thinking to join in the play, held a toilet paper tube so that it extended vertically from her ear. The two-year-old cried out with a perplexed expression and appropriate shaking of her head, "NO! NO!" — which could have meant "this is *my* play, not yours," but in this case meant, "that is not the way you use the 'telephone!'"

Sometimes a part of the child's body can become a symbol. The caregiver will see the child "jogging" her finger across a big wooden block in the center and talking to it as if it were a person. Piaget divided symbols into two categories: symbols and signs. Symbols are personal and created by the child; signs are conventional and used by everyone in that culture. The most common signs are the words of a language. Piaget saw that the young child's use of symbols prepared her to use signs.

These two-year-olds are moving into the preoperational stage, of course, but they still are involved in much sensorimotor play. They seem, at times, driven to find out cause and effect. Stories of the escapades of two-year-olds abound in both homes and centers (unrolled toilet paper, knocked over piles of things...). Ask anyone who works with these children and you will get an example. One two-year-old dribbled honey over the dark blue linoleum of the kitchen floor and then intensely observed household members as they stuck to the floor! Although fun to recall at a later date, it also helps to understand the child because these actions reveal the beginnings of logical thought in the child's mind. "This action causes that result," thinks the two-year-old, Figure 2-22. As the child discovers these cause and effect happenings, he learns to rely on himself instead of being completely dependent on others.

Figure 2-22   Two years — "This action causes that result" is his realization. He plays with his shadow while his mother watches from a distance. *(Courtesy of Pugmire Photography)*

Sol./Comp.	M.B.
Research	4P

Figure 2-23 Two years — The safe design of the playground encourages creativity in spontaneous play. His self-identity becomes more positive as he plays on the raised levels of the outdoor structures.

Constructive play is seen in the toddler's love of poking materials into other materials. They like to mold play-dough and then push craft sticks or similar material into it. Again, as they approach three, they will name this end-product an animal or person.

One of the rewards of working with this age level is the chance to develop play setups or watch for incidents that create positive self-identity in the child's own thinking. This leads to the beginnings of a positive self-esteem that hopefully will grow through the child's lifetime. The child who can successfully manage the steps and then walk on the bridge of a structure in an outdoor play ground feels ten feet tall, Figure 2-23. Recently in our toddler lab, we clapped for a child who had successfully completed a new task in a playful but effective manner. We caught the action with a video camera as the child clapped for herself and then stood a little taller. As the student teachers watched the videotape later, they sat a little taller, too. They realized they had provided the provisions for play that had made this incident possible.

Dr. Sheridan considered that although children of two to two-and-a-half years differ widely in social understanding, the stress of admission to ordinary playgroups and nursery school, without constant availability of very familiar adult caregivers was too burdensome for many children under three years of age. This may be true for many two-year-olds, Figure 2-24, but the hard facts are that over half of the mothers with children under three are in the labor force. (Statistics are from the Bureau of Labor Statistics). As of this writing there were 10.5 million children under the age of six in households where the mother worked outside the home. There are a variety of reasons why growing numbers

Figure 2-24 Two years — Beautiful dreamer! She played so hard she fell asleep. A loving, familiar adult is there to care. *(Courtesy of Ricks College, Toddler Lab)*

of women are entering the workforce; however it is happening. The child care arrangements are varied and include care by friends, neighbors, the other parent, or a relative. Family day-care homes are common. Studies show there are both positive and negative effects produced from different kinds of day-care and from the child being at home through the preschool years. There is still much to be studied. What is apparent is that the best situation for each child and his/her parents must be found and there are many alternatives.

THREE- AND FOUR-YEAR-OLDS

At age three onwards most children are involved in some type of playgroup, Figure 2-25. Groups range from day-care which may be over fifty hours a week to a playgroup that only meets two hours per week. Hopefully all of these provide, under trained guidance, a wealth of opportunity for developing through play competence in everyday skills and ability to communicate effectively with other people. These are the child's keystones of independence as persons and acceptability as personalities.

At three years children still need to play and therefore to learn in small groups, closely attached to one or two familiar adults. During the next year they make rapid strides in socialization, widening their circle of playmates and making less demand for constant attention from members of staff, secure in the knowledge that they are always available when needed. By 4 to 4 1/2 years they may be expected to engage amicably in all sorts of self-directed play activities with three to six age peers, Figure 2-26. At this stage, outdoor, improvised, constructional building, indoor table and floor games, dressing up

Figure 2-25   Three years — Most children are now in playgroups of some sort. Here they enjoy making a chalk mural. Process is more important than product.

and make-believe play are most popular, Figure 2-27 and Figure 2-28. This playing is usually elaborated and carried on from day to day, manifesting an ever-increasing appreciation of the necessity for discussion, planning, sharing, taking turns, and recognition of agreed rules.

From three years with growing command over limbs and trunk and gradual change of shape from toddler chubbiness to school-age slenderness, a child's movements begin to assume that precision, economy, and grace of movement that characterize mature control.

APPLICATION PRINCIPLES

"Let the children play" is our appeal. Both Sheridan, who spent a lifetime as a pediatrician, and Pugmire-Stoy, who has spent a lifetime as an early childhood educator, see the value of allowing children to have the opportunity for many types of play, particularly spontaneous play. As noted, this is also urged in the N.A.E.Y.C. book, *Developmentally Appropriate Practice*. This book presents play as an appropiate medium for learning during these years. Yet, in actuality, many parents and even educators are demanding more and more structured activities for young children. Education is the key. Practical experience as well as research show that children develop to their greatest potential when allowed to PLAY. There is a need to let those involved know of this truth.

Figure 2-26   Four to four-and-a-half years — At this age they play with three to six age peers. The teacher helped focus on a coming local celebration. Complex dramatic play followed.

Cooperative	M.B.
Research	4P

Figure 2-27   Three and four years — The play activities of holidays. The element of play is apprenticeship-to-living. Self-directed activities are important.

Figure 2-28 Four years — Dressing up is an important part of spontaneous play activity. Note the provisions for this play — "the closet" for the dress-up clothes. *(Courtesy of Omega Head Start, Phoenix, Arizona)*

Cooperative	M.B.
App. to Living	4P

He runs freely, climbs over and about the usual nursery apparatus, negotiates slides, crawls through barrels, jumps on small trampolines, and walks on low-placed balance beams, Figure 2-29. He walks up and down stairs, one foot to a step, Figure 2-30, without needing to hold on to a rail, although he is glad to have one of suitable height available.

Figure 2-29 Four-and-a-half years — Child practices her motor skills. Later dramatic play with playmates will involve different types of roles in this setting.

Figure 2-30   Three years — He walks up and down stairs, one foot at a time. Sometimes it is pure skill development; other times it becomes simple dramatic play. *(Courtesy of Ricks College, Toddler Lab)*

He is able to jump down from ever-increasing heights, keeping both feet together and landing without falling. He rides a tricycle, confidently using the pedals and steering safely round sharp corners.

He now has a clear appreciation of space in relation to his own body size and shape, at rest and in movement, Figure 2-31. He has discovered from experience, the spaces where he can pass himself and those where he can navigate with large-wheeled toys such as trucks, dolls' strollers, and Big Wheels, steering forwards, sideways, and backwards. He carries large planks and boards and with the help of cooperative playmates builds houses, cars, space ships, shops, hospitals, and other structures in which to conduct a host of vivid make-believe activities. According to Singer and Singer (1979), who have extensively studied imaginary play, the preschool years are the "golden age of socio-dramatic and make-believe play." (pg. 195). "It reaches full flower in children of four or five and begins a gradual decline at least in overt manifestations" — Figure 2-32 and Figure 2-23. Many other researchers have made similar statements.

Hand skills are also rapidly improving through play with small toys like parquetry blocks, Figure 2-34, jigsaw puzzles, miniature cars, dolls' houses, etc. Both boys and girls enjoy pencil work and cutting out shapes with scissors, although scissor skills often do not develop until the end of the fourth year or into the fifth, Figure 2-35. From threading of

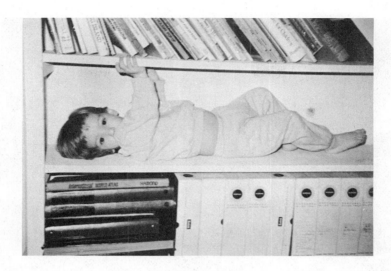

Figure 2-31   Three years — She now has an appreciation of space in relation to her own body, at rest and movement.

Solitary	Pr./Ex.
Occ. Therapy	2P

Figure 2-32   Four years — Building positive self-esteem. An important function of dramatic play.

Figure 2-33   Four years — Role playing includes appropriate noises by a child raised in a farming community.

Figure 2-34   Four years — Hand skills are improving. He creates designs with parquetry blocks. He also likes the homemade classification box (used in many ways).

Solitary	Constructive
Research	2P

Figure 2-35   Four-and-a-half years — Cutting is a favorite activity. Note her concentration. Some are older when they gain this skill and it becomes part of their play.

large beads on laces, then smaller beads on thinner strings, they finally proceed to handling of a large needle in various activities.*

Block building remains popular for many years. Block building proceeds from the simple stereotypes of towers and bridges made of one-inch cubes employed in some preschool psychological tests to highly complicated structures carefully executed with many sizes of unit blocks and auxiliary pieces. These designs are often ingeniously planned and carefully executed. Children of both sexes first employ blocks purely as manipulative objects, then through imitation, copying, and instruction, gradually extend their forward programming or "blueprinting" to the construction of structures which (like their spontaneous drawings) they name beforehand. Later these constructions are often taken into other, more complicated and fanciful play with miniature cars, furniture, and dolls to form part of the settings for dramatic or fantasy play. They are so proud when they have built a really fine block structure. (The block sequence and other sequences are further discussed and pictured in section 3.)

Play with miniature toys becomes more complex. Using accessory pieces like fences or roadways is another example of constructive play. These accessories are used by the child

---

*   *Early sewing and knitting has a cultural basis. In England and elsewhere it is common for five year olds, particularly girls, to do simple knitting and sewing that is actually used in play.*

Figure 2-36   Four years — Play with miniature toys and accessories becomes more complex. He uses constructive play with the accessories, and make-believe with the miniatures.

as he develops stories about the toys. Figure 2-36 shows a traditional doll house and barn scene; these continue to be popular. But there are many miniature toys and buildings of every type available in today's toy market. Children create their own, too. An associate recently contacted me to see if I was emphasizing natural materials in my book about play. She said her fondest childhood memory was making doll furniture from cockleburs (a type of weed with a pod that has spines that stick to everything including other cockleburs). This teacher is very creative in her work and her home. Perhaps her play with miniatures helped her learn about living in a creative way. What could be a better example of a naturalistic setting than a field of cocklebur weeds?

Jigsaw puzzles provide much fun and interest from about 2 1/2 years onwards, although even younger children may enjoy placing shapes in boards with appropriate spaces cut out. Shaped blocks are put in plastic balls or boxes with open configurations in their surfaces. This is only play, of course, if the child is not unduly pressed to perform correctly. Suitable first jigsaws are those in which single colored pictures of some familiar objects are placed in separate matching spaces in a large wooden frame. From three years onwards, puzzles with greater number of places are needed. It is noticeable that many children of this age are more interested in analytic fitting-together of the shapes than building up the picture, so that they will construct it using the plain wooden backs without regard for the attractively colored front picture. Later, assembly of a picture with many more pieces becomes all-important. It is not clear why some children perform in this fashion, but it may be that they are manifesting the commonly found sequence of learning that goes from the simple to the complex. It is interesting to note that many families have adopted "puzzle-doing" as a family play activity. Sometimes separate puzzles with vari-

Figure 2-37   Four years — Play with commercial or homemade play dough is popular. A girl develops skill with a simple tool as she plays. *(Courtesy of Joe Hamilton State Preschool, Crescent City, California)*

ous levels of difficulty are put together by different-aged family members. Other times the entire family will work on one puzzle with a simple part being done by the younger family members. The availability of so many varied puzzles is one of the more interesting play phenomena in our world of today. I view it as an "apprenticeship-to-living" play activity as families or groups of different ages learn to get along together.

Play with commercial clays, play dough, and other moldable materials including the use of real dough in real cooking is much enjoyed at this age and onwards, Figure 2-37 and Figure 2-38. Children especially like making their own doughs following large picture recipes on charts. Although children call this "play" and will often ask the teacher/parent to use the recipe chart on a spontaneous basis, they are doing the "work" of gaining emerging reading skills as they practice following written symbols.

Spontaneous drawing of three- and four-year-olds (as distinct from copy-design which, like writing, is not discussed here) become increasingly elaborate and diverse in color, form and content although still remaining chiefly concerned with people, animals, houses, vehicles, and "designs", Figure 2-39. At first, most of these paintings use only one color. It is frequently disconcerting to a parent who has carefully provided a selection of brightly colored paints or crayons to see their child nonchalantly mixing all the lovely clear pigments together into a mud-colored monochrome and then painting with that, or randomly choosing one crayon with disregard for all the others. Soon the appropriateness of color in relation to whatever visual image the child has in mind delights him.

Figure 2-38   Three and four years — Play with real dough that will be baked is enjoyed at this age. Literacy skills emerge as children follow a picture recipe on a large chart. *(Courtesy of Ricks College)*

Figure 2-39   Three to six years — This is an interesting playspace, but the weather is too hot! Soon they will be inside a cooler house, drawing all kinds of pictures.

Associative	(Later) Constructive
Recreation	4P

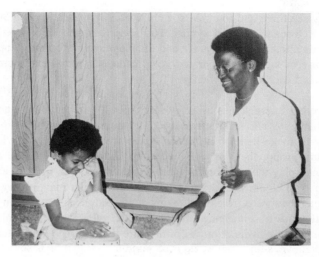

Figure 2-40   Four years — Interest in music-making, usually percussion instruments, shows itself. Often the shy child is helped by music.

Companionate	Games with Rules
Research	4P

At first, the three-year-old does not name his drawing until he has finished. It is not until about four years that he announces beforehand what he is about to draw, indicating that he has some sort of preliminary blueprint in his head before he begins. (These sequences are also further discussed in Section 3.)

Interest in music-making, usually in the form of percussion instruments, generally begins to show itself from about three years, Figure 2-40. Weller-Pugmire says about this stage: "Dramatic play is common. This is seen when the children sing as they play 'house.' Boxes and chairs become trains and planes, and creative movements and rhythm patterns develop. The children play spaceman and sing space songs they have heard.... A cowboy hat leads a child to play cowboy, singing, I'm Goin' to Leave Old Texas Now'" (1977, p.33).

Children with exceptional musical talent nearly always manifest unusually sophisticated tastes very early, not only in their listening, but also in expression, recognizing and recalling tunes learned from adults and older children or heard on various media. Some may ask for and even manage to play such musical instruments as are within their capacity to manipulate. These children, like all other gifted children, deserve every encouragement, but should never be unduly pressed. Proud, affectionate parents of precocious children are particularly open to such temptations to push their children to the extent that the child is not given his deserved opportunities for the spontaneous play of childhood. Spontaneous play gives the gifted and/or talented child great opportunities for learning about living in creative and satisfying ways.

Meanwhile, between three and four years, a child's ability to use spoken language rapidly improves both in vocabulary and syntax. His speech is generally intelligible even to people outside his immediate family. He and his playmates informally communicating in a glorious mixture of words, exaggerated vocal cadences, facial expressions, and telling gestures understand each other perfectly.

By four years verbal interchanges of every sort (friendly, informative, questioning, argumentative, explanatory, and instructive) become increasingly evident in all aspects of play, especially in make-believe situations. Once free communication has been established within any group, the signs of leadership show up clearly, the dominant child deciding who shall play the major roles (such as father, mother, teacher, astronauts, truck driver) and who shall be the subsidiary characters. The leader may or may not generously agree to later interchanges of roles and taking turns. Adult observers can only marvel at the group's meticulous observance of these roles and rules that are mainly unformulated but crystal clear to the players. Nonconformers are soon tacitly eliminated. At this stage a child's make-believe, subjective world is so vivid to him that he is sometimes very hazy concerning what is fact and what is fiction, so that inexperienced caregivers may be startled by his apparently blatant disregard for objective truth. Having simultaneously found their tongues and a broad sense of humor, four-year-olds delight in rhymes, riddles, simple jokes, and verbal teasing.

Children of this age love having stories read to them, especially when they can simultaneously look at the illustrations. Often they will want the same book read over and over. Sometimes they will spontaneously use the characters or the plot from a favorite book in their spontaneous play. Children enjoy guided sessions of "acting out" favorite stories, though. This enriches their spontaneous play later.

The effect of television on children's play is evident to any adult who observes for any length of time in a center or home. The main problem with TV viewing is that it cuts down on the time that children have for spontaneous play (David 1988). Children — some more than others — assume the roles of TV heroes to the exclusion of other types of roles that lead to better problem solving and creativity. There is no general agreement among early childhood educators about allowing or discouraging TV-hero play. If the child has control over his own content of play — and that is the way play is defined in this book — some TV-based play is inevitable. However, if children are provided with other playthings, playspace, and playtime that encourage a wide variety of play, this need not become a problem. Some TV programs are beneficial to the child particularly if he is given adult feedback while watching. Play involving a TV presentation is popular. A mike, a play-screen — Figure 2-41 — dress-up clothes, and/or an overturned rocking boat can quickly become symbolic props that encourage excellent spontaneous play. Sometimes this will be based on TV, but the episodes are briefer and the content of the play has more breadth.

Although three- and four-year-olds now need age-peers to play with, they still enjoy being with their parents and siblings at home, continuing to learn by imitating, trying out new skills, listening, talking, and asking endless questions. It is interesting to note that pretend

Figure 2-41   Four years — Some TV play is inevitable in most situations. A playscreen and well-chosen props often lead to spontaneous TV-based play that has positive content.

play with siblings has a more fanciful content than play with mothers (Dunn 1985). Siblings are likely to be equal partners in play, Figure 2-42.

Three- and four-year-olds particularly like having some special job of their own to do, provided it is not too heavy or too tediously pressed, Figure 2-43 and Figure 2-44. Remember that children like work or "ploy," but work can become drudgery or "slog" even at this early age. It is noteworthy that for gifted children, even more than for other children, the line between play and work or learning barely exists. These children have a desire to be in charge of their destinies, to master the world and to learn learn all the skills for meeting self-imposed challenges....They play what they learn and they learn what they play (Roper 1987). Of course, your author thinks that this statement could be made about almost every child, but she certainly does agree with Roper concerning gifted children.

To review, three- and four-year-olds are in the midst of the preoperational stage. This is the age at which symbolic play often occupies a good deal of the child's free playtime and becomes more complex. They still play with objects, but now they pretend to be grown-ups and soon start announcing their roles ahead of time. Talk on the play telephone becomes the talk of Mom and Aunt Joy; the child will imitate tones and hold the receiver to her doll's ear to share in the conversation. Within a short period, though, she will be joining other children in the housekeeping and block area and there will be assignment of roles ahead of time. There is a flurry of activity as a launching pad is prepared for the rocket. The astronauts get ready at home for the big flight. "I'll be the head astronaut and you can be the crew members," says the leader of this play. Various pieces of material

Figure 2-42   Three and four-and-a-half years — Siblings are likely to be equal partners in play. Mom, upon request, helped them get ready for great make-believe play episodes. *(Courtesy of Nancy Nielson)*

Parallel then Coop.	M.B.
Research	4P

Figure 2-43   Four years — At this age children like some special job of their own, if it is not tediously pushed on them. Look at her positive expression. She knows she is a vital part of her classroom. *(Courtesy of Omega Head Start, Phoenix, Arizona)*

Solitary	Games with Rules
App. to Living	3P

Figure 2-44   Four years — This is the same child shown in Figure 2-35. Now he is doing a special job. Which is work and which is play? Is it Ploy? *(Courtesy of Ricks College)*

from the dress-up shelves become space suits. Troubles with the equipment are straightened out. The influence of TV reports and cartoons can be seen, but the story line is made up and expanded by the children.*

Constructive play is widely used in this age. Although the process is more important than the product, the end results of constructive play often show creativity that is intriguing. Block play continues, but other media such as thin plastic glasses, pieces of styrofoam packing, etc. are often stacked and/or used to create new "things." Molding materials in more complex ways is common. Roads and airport runways are built in the sandbox. The list of end products is inexhaustible.

The parent/caregiver can see the beginning of games-with-rules, but usually it is with an older sibling or playmate. When observed with peers the rules are simple and usually develop from the dramatic play of this stage rather than rules that are announced ahead of time.

Three- and four-year-olds also begin to demonstrate a growing sense of compassion and responsibility. When younger, they appeared to be content to remain detached observers

---

*   *The author documented an incident of "rocket launching play" in the middle sixties when the space-era was beginning. She documented a very similar dramatic play incident at the time the space shuttle "Discovery" was launched in 1988. (See "Letters to Parents," Appendix A)*

of a playmate's hurt or distress. They now show attentive sympathy, running to seek adult help or offering comfort in personal contact or soothing words. They are helpful and protective, although somewhat bossy, towards younger children, particularly their own siblings.

Appetite for adventure is not always matched by appreciation of the dangers of road traffic, swimming pools, and playground equipment. Boys, particularly, seem to benefit less than girls do from verbal appeals, prohibitions, and explanations. It is not clear whether this almost universal characteristic is due to boys' greater courage or to their lesser maturity of foresight; but in relation to accident prevention, adults must continue to be aware of safety at all times for both boys and girls. It is especially satisfying to see playgrounds at centers and backyards at homes where the equipment is safe and the caregiver/parents are diligent in their awareness of safety and adequate supervision, Figure 2-45.

FIVE-YEAR-OLDS

Five-year-olds usually start kindergarten, and that adds a new dimension to their lives, Figure 2-46. Kindergarten sessions are varied throughout the country. Some are part of a day in a day-care center or private school, many are half days in public school, and many are a full or slightly shortened school day. About half of the children still have before- and after-school care from a parent/nanny at home, but there are many other options.

Figure 2-45   Four-and-a-half years — A challenging but safe playspace for solitary play or group play. This ladder also encourages pretense play and FUN!

Figure 2-46 Five years — Kindergarten! These children attend a class where developmentally appropriate practices are followed. Look at their smiles.

Parallel	After Play Time
Research	4P

Sometimes this care is provided within the center or public school. Many private home centers provide this type of care. However, the question of playtime becomes all important. Although most five-year-olds still enjoy symbolic play and gain much from advanced sociodramatic play that they are capable of engaging in, they sometimes are in a combination of school and child-care situations that allow no time for this.

Suggestions for guiding the learning of five-year-olds using developmentally appropriate practice are taken from the book of that name (Bredekamp 1987). Recommendations in the Expanded Edition list suggestions in both the "4-5" year section and the "Primary Grades" section. (This emphasizes an important concept — children should be placed in a group that adjusts to their developmental needs and level rather than in a group that is inappropriately structured by the results of certain tests and screening devices.) Counsel such as "Math skills are acquired through spontaneous play, projects, and situations of daily living" (pg. 71) are used. The reader is urged to study these position statements of the N.A.E.Y.C. Formal research and common sense dictate that children still need many opportunities and time for spontaneous play.

From age five onwards, a child continues steadily to develop her everyday competence and her powers of communication. She has internalized many of the social conventions that are followed in the groups with which she associates. She can show very acceptable manners and yet drop them and be "one of the group" when the occasion warrants it. She has absorbed standards of behavior such as not harming others or taking something that is not hers. Five-year-olds rehearse many of these social conventions in their play scripts (Nelson 1981). They can also take care of a pet, although a parent may still have to check

Figure 2-47   Five years — Her everyday competence and powers of communication can extend to a pet — often a true playmate.

Companionate	M.B.
App. to Living	4P

on this with some children. Often pets are wonderful playmates — true friends — Figure 2-47.

Age five is often called the beginning of the "transitional shift." These children are still in the preoperational stage, but they exhibit more evidence of logical thinking and, of course, are much more advanced than the toddler just entering this stage.

In the social dimension of the play, five-year-olds use all of the categories, of course. Many researchers have studied the social dimensions of play in kindergarten as it relates to gender differences. There seem to be many gender-related factors in the spontaneous social play of five-year-olds. Those who wish to study this more in depth may wish to read studies by researchers such as the Singers, Rubin, Fein, and Kee (see bibliography).

The types of play that five-year-olds use show much more complexity. Constructive play at this age is very common. They still like open-ended materials like plastic shapes, blocks, various types of commercial building toys, or wood scraps of various sizes. They like the woodworking table and can become very proficient in the use of real materials although there must always be sufficient supervision, Figure 2-48. They prefer to make simple constructions using few materials, but evidence of creativity is often shown. No aeronautical engineer has designed planes that are any more innovative in design than many of the five-year-old woodworkers I have supervised. (For me it was the "recreation" element of play — FUN!!)

Figure 2-48   Four and five years — Constructive play shows more complexity. They become proficient at using real tools and materials at the woodworking table. *(Courtesy of Ricks College Preschools)*

Five-year-olds show an increasing enjoyment of elaborate play involving symbolic activities, Figure 2-49. They often handle concerns and even fears with make-believe play. In before- and after-school day-care homes, children will often be observed "playing school." Children will assume personalities of teachers and other children in their classes. There is collaboration between the children as concerns about any part of the school experience are enacted. It is interesting to note how this play differs in content in the before-school play and the after-school dramas on the same day, Figure 2-50 and Figure 2-51.

Five-year-olds are also progressing more into the games-with-rules stage as they participate in indoor and outdoor games that require knowledgeable preliminary instruction, practice, adherence to rules, and an increased sense of fair play.

Some card and memory games are played from one generation to the next. New board games appear regularly. Often the most interesting detail to observe in this game-playing is the way five-year-olds make up their own rules spontaneously. They can create wonderful games-with-rules to be played outdoors. Recreational programs in cities and school districts often feature leagues for five-year-olds in regular games such as soccer and T-Ball. There are some advantages; often whole families participate in these. But, oh! My plea is to encourage five-year-olds to play freely and make up their own games. They do such a fine job when given the opportunity.

All of the elements of play are utilized by five-year-olds, too. Research, apprenticeship-for-living play, and recreation have been discussed before; and I can make the general

Figure 2-49   Five years — Bright plastic interlocking shapes provide excellent opportunities for inventive use and conversation with others.

Figure 2-50   Four to six years — Stress about school situations is being "acted out" in home day-care early in the morning.

Cooperative	M.B.
App. to Living	4P

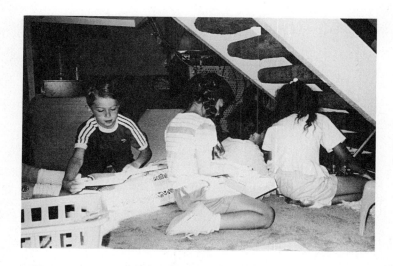

Figure 2-51   Four to eight years — Play continues in after-school day care. Older siblings have joined in the play.

statement that five-year-olds continue using these, Figure 2-52 and Figure 2-53. Now, though, the occupational therapy function is observed more frequently. A child who has just found out that his parents are going to get a divorce will play or draw in ways that reveal his feelings of anger and grief. A child who is bored will play with any material at hand — the lint from the dryer, a stub of an eraser found in the art corner, a skateboard jump on a playground,....The list is endless.

Books and reading are very important to the kindergarten child. Teaching reading in kindergarten is a controversy beyond the scope of this book. I am much more interested in the way books are used in spontaneous play. Meaningful spontaneous play comes from stories in books. Children create "libraries" to play in. Signs are written and posted because of an experience with a book. Again, I can say the list is endless.

Five-year-olds can describe their understanding of friendship. A friend is someone who shares one's playtime. Friends can vary from situation to situation, at home, school, and in the neighborhood. Girls tend to play in small supportive groups, whereas boys tend to play in larger, rough and tumble groups. However, many teachers structure the classroom environment so that boys and girls do play with each other. When there is a bond of friendship formed, whether the friend is the same sex or not, the spontaneous play has a quality of going beyond stereotyped play. The Vehicle of Play can become very expansive and full of vitality.

Figure 2-52   Five years — A well-designed school/community playground encourages skill and/or games-with-rules.

Figure 2-53   Five years — The occupational therapy element of play is observed more frequently. A girl relieves boredom by playing in the rain.

Solitary	Pr./Ex. or M.B.
Occ. Therapy	3P

SIX-YEAR-OLDS

To watch a six-year-old involved in joyous spontaneous play is one of life's experiences to be cherished. Children of this age have such vivid imaginations that show their increased cognitive abilities. Their curiosity and exuberance for living are evident if they are given adequate provisions for play.

The environment of the six-year-old is expanding and so is his energy. He is learning to read and write; therefore he wants to carry out real projects, Figure 2-54. A typical project would be "making secret writing" like she has seen on a video or TV show. On the playground there may be spontaneous active play that involves practicing skills for next year's soccer games or softball that she will begin playing later this year. Notice that girls are playing the games that were traditionally picked as favorites by boys (Sutton-Smith 1979). She is beginning to understand the use of formal rules, but there is still much "bending" to suit her needs.

The six-year-old has personal aptitude for crafts and the creative arts; one can see her constructive skills developing. She makes furnishings and accessories for her dollhouse. This creativity is also evident as she devises games (at home, in school, and on playgrounds) that require no special equipment at all other than the chants and rituals of long unwritten tradition, coupled with lively contemporary improvisations.

Family is still very important to this age and when asked what she likes to do, a six-year-old often makes comments such as "play catch with my brother or find good hiding places

Figure 2-54 Six to seven years — Dad (uncle) puts down his own book to hear his son and nephew read. Later he encouraged spontaneous play about dinosaurs.

Companionate	M.B. (later)
App. to Living	3P (4P later)

Figure 2-55   Six years — They like to play with siblings and cousins. A wonderful spontaneous story is being enacted here with miniature toys and a dollhouse.

with him" — Figure 2-55. Symbolic play is changing, but many six-year-olds still enjoy it in different forms. For example, after school, she may like to get the clothes from the "dress-up box" and act out television commercials.

Not all is completely joyous and exuberant for this age level. They are in the last of the preoperational stage and their minds seem to stretch to try new ideas almost daily. Often they they will try opposite ideas from the day before and often such ideas do not work. They like to play board games, but they are poor losers. Tears are common and those working with this age sometimes sense that the child feels her life is "out-of-balance." Often this can be helped by changing the child's (or children's) environment and having more suitable times and other provisions for play.

Six-year-olds have an increased understanding of time although most do not "tell time" yet. (Granted "telling time" is a skill that some would say is almost obsolete because of digital clocks and watches.) But they can and do learn much through play and can be helped to have a sense of time which helps them realize they need to spend certain periods doing specific tasks; there is still time for the play they want to do. Often they will use the apprenticeship-to-living function of play/work where time is an element. For example, one six-year-old loves to help fix "dinners by candlelight" for special occasions. As the child approaches the age of seven, she seems to be more friendly and cheerful. Perhaps she has learned to handle her expanding environment better and is ready for more advanced challenges. Her world seems more in balance.

SEVEN-YEAR-OLDS

One of my most satisfying periods of teaching came at the end of one year when I was teaching second grade. This group of children worked well together. The ones who were talented in math helped the ones who were slower. If I needed to help a child who had special challenges, the others could busy themselves. We were finished with everything that the state said we had to do and there was a week of school left. "Well," I said, "we can play and we'll do whatever you want to do." This group had its ideas. First we had to convince the custodian that we would clean up the room if we did some "special" things. He agreed and we did clean that room — as we went along. What did the children want to do? Paint and build things! The children made finger paint from various recipes and spread long pieces of paper over the floor and created beautiful murals. We got some old easels and the children painted using various types of brushes and brush substitutes. The children made every type of object imaginable out of "junk material." Many wanted to read a favorite book again. Some wanted to "make books out of scrap paper, and 'stuff' for younger brothers and sisters to use in the summer." We played games outdoors, but we created games with new twists; the second graders made up the rules. A group of happy children left the school that year. After they left, I realized that if I had structured a "review" period, I could not have done as well. The children chose to do activities that strengthened their abilities. They did this by choosing the social dimensions, types, and elements of play that they wanted and needed to use.

That week gave me cause for pondering. It was long before the book *Developmentally Appropriate Practice* was printed. It changed the ways I taught. (I cheered when *Developmentally Appropriate Practice* was adopted as policy by N.A.E.Y.C.!)

I've had opportunities to know some of these second graders as young adults. Invariably they have said, "Remember the week when we played? Oh, that was NEAT...or SPECIAL...or FUN."

An afterword — these grown-up children seem to be relatively happy, productive young adults. Granted, it was only one week with one group in a naturalistic setting. At present I am able to do more controlled research. This research needs to be done; there is much to be learned (Bergen 1988).

Children who have had the opportunity to play spontaneously through the years often exhibit wonderful creativity in many areas as they grow older. The child pictured in Figure 2-56 does not take dancing lessons. She does enjoy watching the modern dance classes at the college where her father teaches. I watched this child dancing in front of a mirror. It was an exceptionally lovely expression of the ways the body can move with the music. I found myself recalling incidents that had taken place several years before when I had witnessed this child and her brother make up stories and act them out with props that they named "play castles," etc. Now, at age seven, this child's creativity is manifesting itself in another way.

Seven-year-olds use more complex forms of active/exercise play; often they use the function of research as they find new ways to use their bodies. Playing different forms of

Figure 2-56   Seven years — She dances spontaneously and creatively. Her movements express exuberance for living.

"tag" is common, as well as developing skills such as climbing on new and more challenging structures, Figure 2-57. They also practice systematically for the games-with-rules that they will play on teams, Figure 2-58. In constructive play, seven-year-olds make more constructions and use more materials, Figure 2-59. There are excellent commercial toys that suit this need, such as Lego-type materials. Children often create their own end products from available materials — even materials found in nature. It is interesting to note that children of this age are becoming more and more interested in miniature toys, micro-toys, etc. Dr. Sheridan was fascinated by the way that children played with miniature toys; I have the same fascination now as do others endeavoring to learn about children. One can learn much about the child by just listening as they play with miniature toys.

Seven-year-olds choose friends of the same sex more and more frequently. They share available play resources with these friends. When asked about their friends, they will infer that a friend is someone who is especially kind to them.

It should be noted that there are some children who often prefer periods of quieter, solitary types of play as they grow older. These children are not always immature. They are sometimes outstandingly creative, the future serious thinkers and academic high-fliers. From an early age, they seem to instinctively realize their need for periods of complete physical and mental relaxation, when they are happier alone in the book corner than on the playground with their more boisterous age-peers, Figure 2-60.

Another particular about the value of spontaneous play can be made as we hear about the fact that Japanese and Chinese students work much harder in school than their American

Figure 2-57   Four years and seven years — Often seven-year-olds use research to find new ways to move their bodies. He enjoys the control he has and is free to express himself with the yell of his current super hero.

Figure 2-58   He practices for his foursquare games perfecting each move. This play led into basketball practice.

Solitary	Pr./Ex.
Research	3P

Figure 2-59   Three-and-a-half to seven years — The older child uses more pieces and makes more complex end products in his constructive play.

Figure 2-60   Almost eight and entering Piaget's concrete operational stage. Her thoughts are more mature. She will still play, but that play will have new dimensions. *(Courtesy of Dr. Veryl Larsen)*

counterparts. Harold Stevenson, University of Michigan psychologist, compared seven thousand students in kindergarten, first, third, and fifth grades in Chicago and Minneapolis with counterparts in Beijing, China; Sendai, Japan; and Taipei, Taiwan. One of his most surprising findings is that "Asian students, contrary to popular myth, are not just rote learners subjected to intense pressure. Instead, nearly 90 perecent of Chinese youngsters said they actually enjoy school and 60 percent can't wait for school vacations to end. These are vastly higher figures for such attitudes than are found in the United States. One reason may be that students in China and Japan typically have a recess after *each* class, helping them to relax and to increase their attention spans" (Butterfield 1990) pp. 4–6.

APPLICATION FOR CAREGIVERS — THE ADULT'S ROLE IN GUIDING PLAY

Some people seem to have an inherent knowlege of ways to help the child in his/her play — including the ability to know when to stay out of the action and when to facilitate the play. However, others need guidelines. Often professionals need to help parents and other caregivers gain this skill. A plan that works with this skill development follows:

1. *OBSERVE.* Knowing the stages that a child goes through in his development will help. Note what the child does with his body, mind, and personality. Sometimes we say to the student teacher, "Let your eyes be a camera, your ears be a tape recorder, and your mind be concentrating entirely on the child and his needs." — Figure 2-61.

2. *CREATE PROVISIONS FOR PLAY.* Structure the environment so that the child has the playthings set up in an effective playspace. Remember that provisions for play do not need to be elaborate or expensive. Choose playthings that are on the child's developmental level. If the child is ready, have some playthings available to encourage him to proceed to more complex play. Again, sometimes we say, "Help the child to stretch if it is developmentally appropriate" — Figure 2-62.

3. *ENCOURAGE SPONTANEOUS PLAY.* Play is the child's vehicle for learning about living. Resist the notion of showing and telling the child what to do. Follow the child's lead. This will lead to ways to build his positive self-identity, Figure 2-63.

4. *FOCUS.* Giving an effective word of praise as he plays in a more complicated play setup, or being the motivator that helps the child move to a more advanced level of play is the skill we wish to develop, Figure 2-64.

5. *LET THE CHILD TAKE CONTROL OF THE PLAY — THAT IS WHAT WE WANT TO HAPPEN!* This leads to true play and the child's gaining the maximum value from that play. (2-81)

Figure 2-61   FIRST: Observe each child carefully. Using your knowledge about the child and about play, determine whether to help him move to more complex play, or to enrich his environment. *(Courtesy of Omega Head Start, Phoenix, Arizona)*

Figure 2-62   SECOND: Create provisions for play that are developmentally appropriate for the child (children) and that are suitable to his (their) particular circumstances. *(Courtesy of Ricks College, Toddler Lab)*

Figure 2-63   THIRD: Encourage spontaneous play. Follow the child's lead; add the plaything that will enrich her play or help her move to more complex play. *(Courtesy of Ricks College, Toddler Lab)*

Figure 2-64   FOURTH: Focus. The teacher helps the child focus by giving effective praise and encouraging him to do more complex play with the pipes. (She also decided to encourage more girls to join in the play with pipes.) *(Courtesy of Ricks College Family Science Dept.)*

Companionate	Constructive
Research	4P

Figure 2-65 FIFTH: Let child take control of the play. Continue observing, etc.

Some Sequences Concerning Spontaneous Play

THOUGHT QUESTIONS

- How can knowledge about the sequences of play aid the caregiver to help the individual child?
- What are the main connections between spontaneous play and language development?
- How can the caregiver use language to encourage play that builds positive self-esteem?

In order to interpret the spontaneous play of children and to understand those players better, the student can study outlines of particular play sequences, both written and pictorial. Obtaining the pictures for this section has been an eye-opener. I have gained much understanding of children and the way they learn about living by being allowed to move through play sequences with the children I've photographed. My students have felt similar benefits as they have photographed play sequences. An "Application for Teachers/Caregivers" follows. I hope that the reader can do this Application and develop pictorial sequeces from and for his/her own center.

PICTORIAL OUTLINES OF PLAY SEQUENCES

Bells and Cups
Solitary practice play is shown as infants amuse themselves (or *work*, as the case may be) with cups and hand bells, Figure 3-1 through Figure 3-5.

Blocks
Constructive (end product) play is shown in the block sequence, Figure 3-6 through Figure 3-13. Like most of the play sequences, many of the types and elements of play can also be seen. Emerging literacy skills are observed as children make signs for their more complicated block structures or ask the teacher to write a story about their creation. Playspace is often an issue with block play because children will build complicated block structures that take more than one session to create. Often these children want to use the structure for spontaneous play that is superb as a setting for role taking, shared social

APPLICATION FOR TEACHERS/CAREGIVERS

Develop your own sequences-of-play pictorial essays. The sequences shown in this section are of two types: (1) spontaneous play with the same toy (example: blocks) taken over several months with the same child or children of different ages; and (2) spontaneous play with similar types of toys/equipment (example: balls) taken of the same child over an extended period or of children of different ages taken in the same period.

Other sequences that can be pictured effectively in addition to those used in this book are:

- woodworking
- any spontaneous play sequences such as "dress-up-and-take-roles" (sociodramatic play)
- play with boxes of different sizes

Some values of this activity are:

- Gaining an understanding of the development of children through play, particularly spontaneous play
- Creating bulletin board material that will be of interest to the children and their parents. (Note: Parents and/or prospective patrons of a center often have time to quickly study and learn from informative bulletin boards when they do not have time to sit down and view a video.)
- Developing a self-help aid that can be studied and added to over one's years in the field of early childhood education. (The process of being involved in such a project helps the E.C.E. (early childhood education) Professional/Advocate be more aware of each child's development through play.)

interactions, problem solving, building of self-identity, etc. (Note: The classic stages of block play as developed by Harriet Johnson are presented using pictures. Solitary to cooperative play can also be seen in this sequence.)

Artistic Performance

This sequence, Figure 3-14 through Figure 3-17, shows motor development as well as symbolic play. An example of parallel play while easel painting and associative or group play while creating a class mural will help the reader see the the value of artistic endeavors beyond the traditional artistic rationales (which are very important, of course).

Figure 3-1 Six-and-a-half months — Grasps bell with both hands, obviously concentrating serious attention on activity. Immediately afterwards she brought the top of the handle to her mouth.

Solitary	Pr./Ex.
App. to Living	3P

Figure 3-2 Six-and-a-half months — She manipulates the bell further and is interested in detail. (Child's handling of the bell is noted in standard developmental scales.)

Figure 3-3   Eight-and-a-half months — She grasps the handle with one hand and playfully bangs it repeatedly on her knee.

Figure 3-4   Eight-and-a-half months — Grasping the cup right side up with both hands, she brings the rim to her mouth.

Solitary	Pr./Ex.
App. to Living	3P

Figure 3-5 Two-and-a-half years — "May I have juice PLEASE?" Cups and other domestic items are incorporated into make-believe play.

Figure 3-6 Stage One — Sixteen months. Ashli carries blocks — domino blocks, unit blocks, or "box blocks" — around the toddler lab. *(Courtesy of Ricks College, Toddler Lab)*

Solitary	Pr./Ex.
App. to Living	4P

Figure 3-7   Stage Two — Building begins with vertical towers. Interlocking blocks are used here, but unit blocks and large plastic blocks are often used. *(Courtesy of Ricks College, Toddler Lab)*

Companionate	Constructive
Research	4P

Figure 3-8   Stage Two — Beginning building also includes horizontal rows on the floor. There is much repetition in construction by these three-year-olds. *(Courtesy of Omega Head Start, Phoenix, Arizona)*

Parallel	Constructive
Research	4P

Figure 3-9   Stage Three — Bridging begins. Often children use problem solving in their spontaneous play to progress to the next stage of block building. *(Courtesy of Omega Head Start, Phoenix, Arizona)*

Associative	Constructive
Research	4P

Figure 3-10   Stage Four — Enclosures: blocks enclose a space. These evolve soon after the child starts building regularly. Note accessories used by some children. *(Courtesy of Omega Head Start, Phoenix, Arizona)*

Figure 3-11   Stage Five — Decorative patterns emerge. Symmetry is often seen. Here an excellent teacher helps the children focus on their play and move to the next level. *(Courtesy of Omega Head Start, Phoenix, Arizona)*

Figure 3-12   Stage Six — A complex block structure is named. The children are proud of their creation. It involved forward planning and precise construction. *(Courtesy of Ricks College)*

Figure 3-13 Stage Seven — The children use their structure for dramatic play. They often label parts of their structure or have a teacher record their story on a chart. *(Courtesy of Ricks College)*

Cooperative	M.B.
App. toLiving	3P

Figure 3-14 Fifteen months — She has a grasp on the pencil down the shaft, and an end product of to and fro lines and dots. Mirror posture in the left hand.

Solitary	Constructive
App. toLiving	3P

Figure 3-15   Twenty-two months — Larger brush work at an easel. Her productions are still more in the nature of visual activities than in representative pictures. She even paints herself.

Figure 3-16   Six and seven years — Spontaneous artistic expression. They decided they want to paint on smooth rocks and can use the family's acrylic paints. The project is skillfully handled.

Figure 3-17 Four-and-a-half and seven years — He draws common environmental objects in his artistic projects. She has a base line for her picture. Both have drawn and colored with playful attitudes and happy concentration.

Doll House Play

Although cognitive development can be inferred in any of the play sequences that are illustrated, simple to complex progression of make-believe play is pictured graphically in the play-with-dollhouses sequence, Figure 3-18 through Figure 3-23. I did not share Dr. Sheridan's enthusiasm for dollhouse play as a method of learning more about children and their development. Certain reviewers did share her belief; for that I give professional acknowledgement. I heeded my own advice, did the "Application" (on page 90), and have become a great advocate of dollhouse play. Sometimes the teacher/caregiver can join in the play — particularly with a child who has a personal problem — and gain insight into the child's emotional and social beliefs about himself. This may give the teacher/caregiver valuable information to help the child develop positive self-esteem.

Some have expressed the challenge that dollhouse play is no longer representative of children's play in America. I might have said that, too, before I started surveying homes, E.C.E. Centers, and toystores. There are many types of dollhouses other than the traditional ones. Some of these houses, of course, are the ones made by children out of shoe boxes, etc. — spontaneous play. Those are great! But there are many other types of dollhouses and play with them follows the same general outline as pictured in this sequence.

Figure 3-18   Three years — This boy assembles meaningful groups near but to the outside of the dollhouse, talking to himself continuously.

Solitary	M.B.
Recreation	3P

Figure 3-19   Three-and-a-half years — She places some miniature toys in the dollhouse, but plays mostly in front of the dollhouse. She looks to see if others are appreciating her play.

Figure 3-20   Four years — He uses imaginative placement of miniature accessories. Stories start to emerge. These tell about events in/on the house.

Figure 3-21   Four-and-a-half years — Now the miniature furniture is arranged within the doll-house. Classification of toys is shown. She plays constructively in all rooms of the house.

Figure 3-22   Seven years — Note the position of the hands. These girls are using needles and thread to make curtains for the dollhouse, as they play inside on a snowy day.

Parallel	Constructive
App. to Living	4P

Figure 3-23   Seven-and-a-half years — Now he can follow directions as he assembles dollhouse accessories. He has a boost in self-esteem as he realizes he can do this.

Figure 3-24   Three years — He gets out all the miniature toys, but there is no set order to his playing.

Solitary	Constructive
Research	3P

Miniature Toy Play

Dr. Sheridan felt that much could be learned about children by listening to their comments and watching their actions as they played with miniature toys. I heartily agree. The miniature toys pictured in this sequence, Figure 3-24 through Figure 3-28, are simple wooden shapes. In taking photographs, I learned much about the development of children, as did their parents/teachers who were watching. In the past months, miniature toys have flooded the toy market. Of course, one needs to select these for safety and make certain they are developmentally appropriate for the age being used. Personally, I like the plain, wooden, miniature toys best. However, my associates and I are intrigued with the language interaction possible with the individual child, including the child with special needs, as each plays with these small toys.

Puzzles

This sequence, Figure 3-29 through Figure 3-32, shows simple to complex play. One can see physical, cognitive, social, and emotional development in the child as puzzles are put together. These pictures all show solitary play, but often people work together to get puzzles put together.

Ball Play

Many readers will relate personally to the "ball play" sequence, Figure 3-34 through 3-40, because those involved in early childhood education realize that the ball is usually one of the child's first and most beloved toys. Involvement with balls and ball games extends

Figure 3-25   Five years — The shopping mall she constructed occupies the most prominent place in her layout. Other toys have random placement, but she plays with cars freely.

Figure 3-26   Six years — His town is more artistically and realistically arranged. He talks with his sister as he lands a plane on the roof of a building.

Figure 3-27   Eight years — Note thoughtful concentration. He planned the entire layout before he started playing with the toys.

Figure 3-28   Three to eight years — "Oh, can we play together now?" asked the family members. The group story and make-believe play was fun to watch and hear.

Cooperative	M.B. & Constructive
Recreation	4P

Figure 3-29   Two years — She can name most of the objects on the puzzle pieces and twist her wrist to get each piece in the right place.

Figure 3-30   Two-and-a-half years — He can put together a slightly more advanced puzzle now. He contemplates where the pieces will go.

Figure 3-31 Three years — He is well able to cope with this more complicated jigsaw puzzle, although its large size required unhurried contemplation.

Figure 3-32 Six years — He puts a complicated puzzle together just "in passing," as he leaves the school room.

Figure 3-33   Fifteen months — His main word is "BA" (ball) and he spontaneously plays with an older child's basketball set.

Figure 3-34   Three years — Although able to kick a large ball gently, she is still unable to coordinate eyes, arms, and hands to catch a smaller ball. Her whole posture is age-characteristic of girls.

Figure 3-35   Three-and-a-half years — He is developing skill in handling a ball. Notice that he is using his big brother's glove (symbolic prop).

Figure 3-36   Three-and-a-half years — His whole body is actively engaged as he throws the ball.

Figure 3-37   Three years, nine months — Boy's running approach to a kick. His entire attention is harmoniously coordinated.

Figure 3-38   Three years, nine months — Anticipating the catch. Note the head-body posture and anticipatory position of legs, arms, and hands. This is age-characteristic for boys.

Figure 3-39   Four-and-a-half years — He practices with a T-ball stand at home, anticipating the time he can be on the city recreation teams.

Solitary	M.B.
Research	3P

throughout the lifetime of most individuals, although for some it is a more active involvement and for others it is more passive. Many parents will relate to a sequence of ball play pictures. This type of sequence is often a way to teach parents more about the natural development of play.

Puppet Use

This sequence, Figure 3-40 through Figure 3-41, shows play that can be companionate with mother/teacher, or can illustrate any of the social dimensions of play (solitary, companionate, parallel, associative, or cooperative.) However, the student of this book is urged to think of the language development that is taking place in this series of pictures.

Computer Use that Leads to Spontaneous Play

This section, Figure 3-42 through Figure 3-45, shows an actual sequence of spontaneous play I observed. This type of play evolved from the professions of the parents in the homes of the children with whom I am most involved. This sequence does not necessarily intend to recommend use of computers in early childhood education; that is a philososphical decision of individuals. The sequence could just as well be on doctor/nurse play, grocery clerk play, truck driver play, etc. The point is that children very often play spontaneously using their interpretations of their parents' occupations as a theme.

Figure 3-40   Fourteen months — The puppet evokes delighted vocalization and she is anxious to share her excitement with her mom.

Companionate	M.B.
Recreation	4P

Figure 3-41   Three and six years — Brothers practice communication skills as they make two puppets "talk." Great indoor fun when its too hot to play outside.

Figure 3-42   Three years — Both of his parents work with computers. His self-identity soars when he is allowed to play on the computer. Mom is nearby.

Comp. or Solitary	Games with Rules
App. to Living	4P

Figure 3-43   Three-and-a-half years — Now he shows a cousin how to play a computer game.

Figure 3-44   Six years — They had been playing a game on the computer that had "levels." They created their own spontaneous game-with-levels based on the computer play. Note the tongue being used as a symbolic prop.

Figure 3-45   Six and seven years — Note those looks of positive self-identity. They pretend they are grown-up computer workers.

THE STAGES OF COMMUNICATION DEVELOPMENT AND ITS RELATIONSHIP TO SPONTANEOUS PLAY*

AGES	MANIFESTATION	STAGES
2–3 mo.	Reception	Returns stares to caregiver; turns head to voices.
2–3 mo.	Expression	Coos (vowel-like sounds) — often in response to the caregiver's interactions; responds to caregiver's singing and humming with body movements; gives the true social smile.
3–4 mo.	Reception	Awake longer and is more responsive to caregivers.
3–4 mo.	Expression	Cooing and gurgling; whole body can become responsive in companionate play; starts to chuckle, especially when involved in an activity such as being bounced on a knee; sucks on hand (it's handy and he is in charge!); tries to put everything in the mouth; plays with tongue and saliva.
4–6 mo.	Reception	Pays obvious interested attention to close-by, meaningful sounds, particularly familiar voices.
	Expression	Vocalizes responsively when spoken to face-to-face; babbles to self and others using a sing-song intonation with single or double syllables; Babbling can be identified as sound-play that is spontaneously produced; toe-play ("this little pig went to market") elicits cooing that often sounds like actual "responses" to companionate players.
6–8 mo.	Reception	Immediately attends to and localizes nearby, everyday, meaningful sounds, particularly human voices; beginning to respond dis-

---

*   *The stages of language development and their relationship to play (including spontaneous play) has been researched extensively. Those who wish to study language development in more depth are referred to Early Childhood Experiences in Language Arts by Jeanne Machado (Delmar Publishers, Inc.). Specific research on language development as it relates to spontaneous play is cited in the bibliography.*

criminatively to emotional overtones in speech of familiar adults (i.e., soothing, prohibitive, etc.).

	Expression	Babbles continuously to self and others in long, tuneful, repetitive strings of syllables with wide range of pitch and consonant sounds; beginning to imitate adults' playful vocalizations in face-to-face situations, such as when a caregiver makes a noise the baby has just made (this often causes laughter); starts making gestures and reaches out to return playful touches; often develops mannerisms of playfulness when caregiver responds.
8–12 mo.	Reception	Seems to want to imitate the sounds adults make, but is seldom successful; Understands words like "no, no" and simple commands better; recognizes names of specific personal objects (example: "book" means his favorite book, not all books).
	Expression	Plays interactive games like "peek-a-boo"; will playfully talk to himself while looking in a mirror; uses babbling to repeat "words" and syllables over and over again (this is called "echolalia" and seems to be a form of solitary play); points to large pictures in a favorite book; plays with objects like a bell or a musical ball and imitates the sounds; seems to be talking when he plays, especially as he expresses emotions; starts using "Ma-ma" and "Da-da" (this happens in every culture); usually says another "first" word around twelve months; this begins the symbolic functioning of words and opens up many avenues for spontaneous play.
12–18 mo.	Reception	Responds appropriately to meaningful, everyday sounds within a close range; recognizes own and family names and words for several common objects and activities; sensitive to expressive cadences in speech of her family members and other caregivers; responds to names of body parts when named in an action poem or chant.

	Expression	Jabbers continuously to self and others employing loud, tuneful jargon (the holophrase — a single-word utterance that the young toddler combines with gestures and intonations — does the work of a whole sentence as the child plays); uses many symbolic gestures that reveals she understands many words; ekes out communication difficulties with urgent intonations and finger pointings (often this is the reaction to "cause and effect" noticed by the toddler in her play); takes part in family/group amusement activities, such as watching a sibling's or parent's ball game or participating in a "carnival" at an early childhood center by imitating noises and gestures.
18–24 mo.	Reception	Shows clearly by correct response to spoken communications that she hears and understands many more words than she can utter.
	Expression	Speaks twenty to fifty or more single words and is beginning to join two words that are subject/predicate ("Truck go") or topic/comment ("Fries good!") in nature. (This is often heard in simple symbolic, research, and apprenticeship-to-living play). Refers to self by name; sometimes words sound unintelligible to caretakers and almost always to strangers; the child does have playful linguistic interchange with caregivers; often echos final or stressed word in sentences/questions addressed to her; beginning to play meaningfully with miniature toys and domestic objects.
2–3 yrs.	Reception	Comprehends the meanings of most nouns and verbs as well as the function of objects; points to almost any object when named; speaking vocabulary goes from fifty or more words to approximately five hundred words during this year, but he understands a great many more.
	Expression	"NO!" is the word associated with this stage; even when starting to combine words, he will say "No play ball!"; "MINE" is another word that expresses a strong personal opinion during play; begins to use possessive forms, such as "Yeggi's doll"; phrases and questions (both ask-

ing and answering) are heard in dramatic play episodes; likes simple games involving words that call for actions like, "Jump!" and simple songs that have actions using both sides of the body; books are used as attention getters; two-year-olds realize that they can control the caregiver as they respond to being read to and talked with (this has many positive aspects, of course); word invention is used as the child approaches three — for example, one boy asked only for a "biganared" for Christmas, and sure enough, the gifts he played with the most were red boxes, the bigger the better.

3–4 yrs.	Reception	Comprehends literal meanings of words and is beginning to appreciate common language variations, such as the different meanings of words and how they relate to the real world (semantics).
	Expression	Echolalia persists; vocabulary rapidly enlarging; uses sentences of three to five words, personal pronouns, and most prepositions; talks continuously to self at play; often makes up his own songs; infantilisms of articulation and grammar gradually diminishing; intelligible even to strangers; asks many questions (Who? What? Where?); engages in make-believe play alone or with one or two others; plays meaningfully with miniature toys providing simultaneous running commentary to herself or whoever will listen; play with words begins — for example, three-year-old Matt went with his grandparents to pick raspberries. As they headed home, a Ray Bradbury story was on the radio. Matt started saying, "Raspberry, Bradberry, Mattberry, Grandmaberry, Grandpaberry," etc., etc. — all the way home — using every name in extended family. This was the recreational element of play as well as language play. True fun!
4–5 yrs.	Reception	Competent for most everyday situations, provided sentences are not longer than six to seven words and vocabulary employed reflects the child's experience.

Expression

Uses large vocabulary with conventional grammar and syntax (arrangement of words); articulation still shows residual infantilisms but speech is usually intelligible even to strangers; narrates long stories and uses language extensively in elaborate play episodes; asks numerous questions (especially "WHY?") and asks the meanings of words; sings more complex songs and often makes up words to go with the beat of rhythm instruments; draws pictures of people, houses, transport, and other common objects; likes to tell stories about his drawings and have the teacher write his words on the paper (often this will lead to play or be the result of play; signs for block constructions and miniature toy arrangements are developed in the same way); word play — often absurd and nonsensical to the untrained ear — is common; children interact with their "silly" answers and word capers. (Most parents have stories about their children saying "hangerburger" or something similar for "hamburger." But when the children are playing "Fast Food Place" in dramatic play they will start with "hangerburger" which goes on to "slangerburger" to "tangerburgly" and so on. Part of the fun is in the control of the language, of course, and the ability to garble the words seems delightful to children. This actually shows the child's skill in using language. Friendship during play can now be influenced with words. Children can be included or excluded from the play with words or signs.)

5-6 yrs.   Reception

Completely competent for all home, school, and neighborhood situations; understands passive speech (The girl was hugged by her teacher); can listen effectively when she wants to and this listening leads to playful exchanges of communication; can follow complex directions;

Expression

Spoken language fully intelligible, grammatical, and fluent; engages in elaborate make-believe play and win/lose team games with chosen friends, explaining rules and objectives lucidly; draws more elaborate pictures showing people and objects in all sorts of everyday situations; interested in learning to read, write, and calculate; participates in chants of childhood such as jump rope rhymes and loud counting or challenges that are part of children's traditional games; uses language extensively in puppet play and dramas and playacting of various types; knows many songs and often creates words to go with music she likes.

Figures 3-46 through 3-52 show some of the aspects of communication that go beyond the child's actual talking and listening in play. Gestures, imitation, extending of empathy between players, etc., have their place. Interested teachers and parents further emerging competency in many ways.

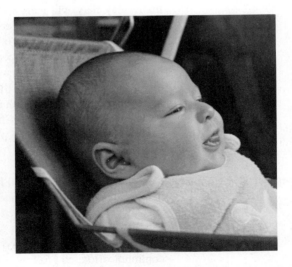

Figure 3-46   Six weeks — The infant plays with his tongue. He gets a pleasant sensation so he does it again.

Figure 3-47 Two years — Gestures and imitation are an important part of communication, and communication is an important part of living. *(Courtesy of Nancy Nielson)*

Figure 3-48 Three years — She is learning English rapidly — sometimes by listening instead of talking, as she plays or does body action poems.

Figure 3-49 Three and six years — Explaining about something that happened while playing. The reception appears to be excellent.

Figure 3-50 Five years — Much communication is learned as teacher gives directions and child follows. *(Courtesy of Joe Hamilton State Preschool, Crescent City, California)*

Figure 3-51 Student teacher Kaylene has made a device to help her students learn the 911 phone number. (They use a real phone too.) This led to later spontaneous play and improved language skills. *(Courtesy of Ricks College)*

Figure 3-52 Patient parents, observing, listening, and waiting. They learn much about their child as they take part in a parent involvement activity. *(Courtesy of Joe Hamilton State Preschool, Crescent City, California)*

APPLICATION FOR CAREGIVERS[*]

Have a teacher or classmate do a "Language Development through Play Observation" for you. Note that language development is pictured in the trunk of our Vehicle of Play. (My students have also suggested that they like to think of language as the "wing" on a racing vehicle. That wing helps the racing vehicle go forward more effectively!)

Procedure:

1. Both you and your observer/helper will need to study the following coding:

    -   A.M. — Adult Modeling — Caregiver sets positive example of effective speech, expressions, gestures, open-ended questions, and listening

    -   C.I. — Child Initiates — Caregiver listens and, by effective pauses and encouraging expressions, lets the child begin the conversation and learn turn-taking in speech.

    -   E.P. — Effective praise, especially the well-earned variety. This type of praise by the caregiver builds positive self-esteem in the child.

    -   S/F/P — Singing, fingerplays, and/or poems that build vocabulary and teach other components of communication.

2. Have your observer watch you for thirty to forty minutes as you interact with the children. Observer writes the appropriate code and then records exactly what you do and say.

3. Study the completed form with your observer and discuss how you could be more effective in your guiding of children to help them gain effective communication skills.

---

[*] *This observation can also be done for a child development class assignment. In this case, the student observes any parent/teacher in a naturalistic setting and adapts the procedure above to report communication skills.*

Play for Exceptional Children

THOUGHT QUESTIONS

- How can applying knowledge about the framework of play help a caregiver see the assets and needs of exceptional children?
- What are some specific ways to encourage spontaneous play in the handi-capable child?
- How can a person determine ways to help the special needs child advance to the next level of play?

A colleague in our department returned from a William's Syndrome Convention with a series of buttons which she had pinned on a banner for safekeeping (and a laugh). The buttons said, "Mildly Normal, Moderately Normal, Severely Normal, and Profoundly Normal." She was not surprised at the comment these caused — some of it humorous and some of it serious and philosophical (with good reason). Hopefully we are moving away from the time when the child was branded with set labels that stereotyped the possible development of abilities and talents within the individual person. Hannah, the professor's daughter with William's Syndrome, has learning difficulties severe enough that when her Individualized Educational Plan (IEP) was formulated the last time, it was determined that she would do best in a self-contained classroom (a classroom for exceptional children only, within a regular school building) during most of the day and mainstreamed in a regular classroom during the rest of the day. In a year or two, Hannah's education team anticipates she will be ready to be mainstreamed in a regular classroom the entire day. This child is loved by her family, neighbors, and older friends in a special way; she has a great capacity for friendliness. One of my students who did a case study through the observation windows of the Child Labs when Hannah was in our nursery school, gained an insight into her own socialization skills which she greatly desired to improve. This intellectually-adept college student credits Hannah with showing her ways to make and keep friends which improved her life. She titled her case study, "So Who Is Normal?"

William's Syndrome children have a distinctive appearance and are sometimes called "Pixie People." (There was a TV special by this name that helped many parents be aware that William's Syndrome might be their child's problem.) Although Hannah had been diagnosed when the TV special was aired, her case is fairly typical. She was a low birth weight child, but the parents were told that she would "catch up." Hannah was about a year old when she was finally diagnosed. Her pediatrician had never seen a case before.

Hannah's parents found a support group in a neighboring state; this has been a help to them. William's Syndrome children have been noted to be extremely friendly and talkative. Mental retardation of various degrees is a common feature (Goodman and Gorlin 1983, page 318).

Field-working health personnel, teachers, parents, and grandparents know that the range of possible accomplishments for successful living is wide; limits are difficult to define, especially for the child with special challenges. (That is why myself and others like to use the term handi-capable.)

One finds that there is disagreement concerning the words that are used to describe those with special needs. The word *handicapped* is used in public laws such as PL 94–142 and PL 99–457. Therefore, the word "handicapped" is accepted as official in many situations. Its general use means that a person has a condition that causes problems when interacting with various environments. The condition may be physical or mental or it may be social and/or emotional so that it causes challenges with interpersonal relations. A person may be handicapped in one circumstance, but not in another. As a child, Hannah was handicapped in some of her motor abilities, but not in her social interactions, Figure 4-1. As an older child, she no longer is handicapped in most situations requiring motor skills. Sometimes, though, she feels rejected in the classroom where she is mainstreamed part of the day (the term "social isolate" is often used to describe this), Figure 4-2.

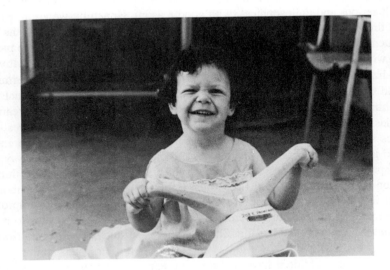

Figure 4-1   Three years — Hannah is a William's Syndrome child. She is extremely friendly and talkative in her play, but she has had some gross motor challenges. Play on big-wheeled toys has helped.

Figure 4-2 Nine years — At present Hannah is still very friendly, but is often a social isolate in the classroom where she is mainstreamed part of the day. She chose to play "Simon Says" with other children in her contained classroom.

The words *impairment, disability* and *challenge* are often used to describe specific problems. An example would be using the terms "physically impaired" or "physically challenged" to refer to an accident victim who needs to use a wheelchair to get around. The term "exceptional children" is used with those who "differ from the norm — either below or above — to such an extent that an individualized program of special education is required to meet their needs. This term *exceptional children* includes both children who experience difficulties in learning and children whose performance is so superior that special education is necessary if they are to fulfuill their potential" (Heward and Orlansky 1988, page 3). These "gifted" children have been referred to earlier in this text. When I use the term "exeptional children" in this section, I will be referring to those with disabilities/impairments.

The norms of growth and development as presented in section 2 must be understood in order to understand the growth pattern of children who are not developing in the usual manner. With this kind of understanding, it is possible to plan better for the child with disabilities and problems. It is also possible to better identify those areas where the handicapped child's needs and abilities are the same as those of other children, because all children need to be cared for, loved, and have a feeling of self-worth.

There is general agreement that all early learning is related to increasingly effective integration of sensory and motor experience. These learning experiences are themselves the result of imitation and constant practice of well-established adult usages. Consequently, children with any serious defect of vision, hearing, locomotor equipment, or central nervous system functioning, which interferes with the normal organization of sensory intake and motor output, are at a disadvantage compared with their normal age-peers. They often have trouble gathering a working knowledge of the ordinary world. For this reason they must be encouraged to make best use of whatever assets they possess, while at the same time ensuring that they continue with activities designed to reverse or control the effects of impairments.

In the United States, this has become more of a reality as federal legislation has been implemented. The Education for All Handicapped Children Act (PL 94–142) is sometimes called the "Bill of Rights for Handicapped Children." Signed into law in 1975, this law provided that all handicapped children have available to them a free and appropriate public education. Education in the "least restrictive" setting is the term used to describe this directive. If possible, children are entitled to the opportunity to participate in every activity that is available to everyone else. This includes placement in a regular classroom (with an aide, if needed). This has come to be called *mainstreaming*. Mainstreamed children are in a regular classroom for as much of the school day as is feasible. Some spend part of the day in a special "resource" room where trained personnel can help them with their challenges. Another important part of the law was a special preschool incentive grant. This incentive money was used to encourage states to provide education and related services to preschool handicapped children (ages three to five.) In 1986, an amendment to PL 94–142 was passed, PL 99–457.

Amendment H mandates that by 1991 all states *must* serve developmentally delayed, disabled, and high-risk three-, four-, and five-year-olds. In addition, there is discretionary legislation that gives money to states to find and serve children from birth to age three and to plan the most beneficial program for them. Handicapped children younger than three need to be identified in order to receive this assistance. Those who have known that the earlier a child is identified and effectively helped, the greater are his/her chances for a fulfilled, contributing life, applauded this development. The data showed that early identification and intervention proved to have significant cost effectiveness. This was a significant factor; there is wide use of this discretionary legislation. New types of workers have become needed who have an understanding of the very early childhood of children with special needs. An example is the "caseworker" who will work with the family after the child's IFSP (Individualized Family Services Plan) has been formulated. In fact, this will affect some workers in the fields of education, medicine, social services, and nutrition as they work with these youngest children.

The Individualized Education Program (IEP) is a statutory requirement of PL 94–142. It is a plan for the education of the grade schooler that is formulated by the child's teacher and parents (or guardian) and even the child, on some occasions. Other professionals who can help the child are sometimes included in the development of the IEP. In states which used the preschool incentive program before PL 99–457 was passed, IEPs were often used for preschool children, also. Much learning has occurred both for professional teachers and parents as concerned individuals have learned to develop effective IEPs. It was established that careful assessment to pinpoint the child's skills and deficiencies was a necessity. Then annual goals were determined. These goals were divided into short-term, instructional objectives that could be measured and accomplished within a certain time framework. Usually these short-term objectives were arranged in sequence in order to reach the annual goals. Knowledge of the way that handicapped children grow through play — particularly spontaneous play — is vital as parents and professionals develop these learning plans.

The family is recognized in PL 99–457 as the central agent in a special-needs child's life to help that child reach his/her maximum potential. The Individualized Family Service Plan (IFSP) is written with the family and the child study team.

THE PLAY OF HANDICAPPED CHILDREN

As noted in previous sections, young non-handicapped children in all their playtime engagements are eager learners, showing strong drive and concentration. They have a compelling urge to know and to do. Having mastered any basic skill, they spontaneously go forward, devising additional complexities and difficulties in task performance and then working hard to overcome them. When they recognize the need for knowledgeable outside assistance, they actively seek it.

Dr. Sheridan noted in her practice and studies that many children with special needs have conditions that are unrelated to intelligence or motivation. But she also became aware that there are many types of exceptional children who are slow learners. In contrast to their age-peers, some may lack drive and powers of concentration. Having achieved a basic skill, they may tend, unless continually encouraged toward new goals, to continue in the same stage indefinitely or gradually to relax and regress. They seldom appreciate the necessity to seek outside help by themselves, but sometimes just give up trying. In order to progress, they require patient, individual, step-by-step instruction and must be gently but firmly stimulated to constant practice.

This step-by-step instruction and constant practice is what many of the short term goals in the IEPs seek to accomplish. Even seemingly unpromising handicapped children, by reason of biological, maturational factors alone, may be expected to gain some forward progression, although their developmental gains may be uneven, fluctuating, and dissociated. Physically impaired children with normal intelligence and stable personalities often show a rewardingly rapid response to appropriate therapies. Often they show exceptional powers of concentration and perseverance as they devote themselves to the attainment and practice of gross motor skills, eye-hand coordination, and interpersonal communication (although not always in spoken words). Instinctive biological drives, however, can only take the most strongly motivated children a certain distance. Owing to their limited opportunity for exploration and exploitation of their environment in the early years of life, all subsequent developmental stages tend to be delayed and/or prolonged unless early intervention is provided.

Some children with developmental delays are in early childhood programs such as Project Head Start. Others have been placed in special programs in settings such as regional Child

Development Centers. However, others are not receiving help nor are their parents being given the training and support that they need in order to effectively help these children at home. With the implementation of PL 99–457, this situation should improve. However, as stated before, there needs to be more awareness of the needs of these very young children, especially how they can learn through play — the heritage of every child.

> Your author spends time in big cities (as a speaker, consultant and visitor) as well as in rural areas which surround the town where her college is located. Often I hear the statement, "These handicapped children are identified at birth or soon after by medical personnel." This is not always true. Although I have the highest regard for medical workers, some young children with handicapping conditions are not identified, especially in the rural areas of our country. Some handicapping conditions become evident months after birth; some are caused by accidents, injuries, and regrettably, child abuse. I cannot emphasize strongly enough the urgency of finding every child that needs help in the early years.

> Many of these children can be helped at home; their parents will be given the training. Hopefully, with projects such as those that are usually called "Child Find" or some similar title, these children can be identified and receive the help they need.

The Vehicle of Play Framework can be used to show that children with special needs are able to learn about living in their world through play, too. Now it is acknowledged that almost every child can learn if the individual has appropriate education in the appropriate environment. Most of those who work with special-needs children will agree that an individual child can learn through play although she may need to be taught and encouraged to move from one level of playing to the next. Young handicapped children are also entitled to pleasurable use of a portion of their time during which they have some control, at the least, of their activities.

With this thought as a guideline, I would like to present the Framework of Play using pictures of exceptional children. As stated above, the range of handicapping conditions varies widely; yet using the Framework will help us appreciate the role of play in the life of the specific child or group of children.

Social Dimensions of Play

To review, this is the child's capacity for socialization (interacting with other people). The new dimension of play that I have added to Parten's classification, *companionate play*, is often used with children with special needs.

ONLOOKER — A mentally retarded child (he was a twenty-seven-week "preemie") is watching his foster father play with another child. Dad will encourage him to join in the play knowing he likes play involving music; this child has perfect pitch — an asset! (Figure 4-3.)

SOLITARY — A four-year-old girl has Turner's Syndrome; she is small for her age. She attends preschool and is learning rapidly. She loves to play! (Figure 4-4.)

Figure 4-3   Onlooker play by a severely mentally retarded boy. (He was a twenty-seven-week "preemie.") His dad will encourage him to join the play. *(Courtesy of Walton Foster and Day Care Home, Idaho Falls, Idaho)*

Figure 4-4   Four years — Solitary play by a girl with Turner's Syndrome. Her teacher watches her play and says "She is doing well." *(Courtesy of Joe Hamilton State Preschool, Crescent City, California)*

Figure 4-5 COMPANIONATE — This child was a "near drowning" victim. He has multiple challenges. He does enjoy being swung. (The student teacher checked with her supervisor before starting this play.) *(Courtesy of Ricks College Respite Labs)*

COMPANIONATE — A student teacher plays with a severely handicapped child who loves to be swung back and forth. She looks and listens for cues in order that she can help him take at least some control of the play. He enjoys this greatly! (Figure 4-5.)

PARALLEL — Children in a foster-care home enjoy jumping on the trampoline together although there is no real interaction. (Each child has different impairments.) (Figure 4-6.)

ASSOCIATIVE — Aerial view of sandbox play in preschool. Children with language delays enjoy the play with the others, of course. The teacher finds that this play is a good opportunity to extend language development. The children are still learning other things about living and are having fun. (Figure 4-7.)

COOPERATIVE — Several children are involved in the dramatic play area of a Head Start program. Note the teacher in the background who is extending the language of a child. Language is encouraged as the children take various roles. (Figure 4-8.)

Types of Play

To review, remember that this wheel of the Framework of Play shows the developmental aspects of play and emphasizes cognitive development. Although the play starts during a definite age and stage in most children without handicapping conditions, once it starts, the play usually extends throughout the person's lifetime. The play, of course, develops into differing and more complex forms.

Figure 4-6   Two and five-and-a-half years — Parallel play of children in a foster care home. They're enjoying the side-by-side play. (They are well supervised, of course.) *(Courtesy of Walton Foster and Day Care Home, Idaho Falls, Idaho)*

Figure 4-7   Four years — ASSOCIATIVE PLAY. Language delayed children enjoy the play. Teacher encourages conversation and asks open-ended questions. *(Courtesy of Joe Hamilton State Preschool, Crescent City, California)*

Figure 4-8 Four to five years — COOPERATIVE PLAY. Note teacher in background extending the language of a child. Other children are involved in dramatic play. *(Courtesy of Omega Head Start, Phoenix, Arizona)*

Children with certain types of handicaps will often have to be encouraged and taught to progress to the next stage of play. Since some types of play require different degrees of abstraction, which is a higher level of cognitive development, not all children with impairments are able to advance to the higher levels. However, many can.

PRACTICE/EXERCISE — This two-year-old child, who had spinal meningitis at eight months, had to "start over at day 1" said his teacher. He spends time in front of a special mirror. His actions are growing in complexity and he seems to enjoy the activity. He also "sings" with the music playing in the center. (Figure 4-9.)

CONSTRUCTIVE — A speech-delayed child in a preschool uses miniature toys and pieces of wood to form patterns on a turntable. In this case, the miniature toys are a construction device because there is an end product emerging. Teacher Marsha will get child to talk about her product to her friend who is parallel playing beside her. This will help with her speech. (Play will become associative play.)

MAKE-BELIEVE — This child has severe impairments as the result of an automobile accident. She has received much help from various sources, but has permanent mental impairment. She really enjoys the make-believe play of the much younger child; she enjoys playing with younger children. Her parents are creating a special environment for her where she will have facilities that are appropriate for her and where she can use pleasurable activities to gain competence in everyday skills. (Figure 4-10.)

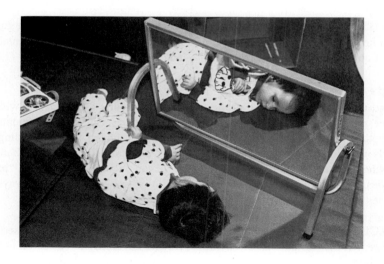

Figure 4-9 Two years — PRACTICE/EXERCISE PLAY. Child who had spinal meningitis plays in front of mirror. His actions are becoming more complex! *(Courtesy of Health & Welfare Child Developmental Center, Region 7, Idaho)*

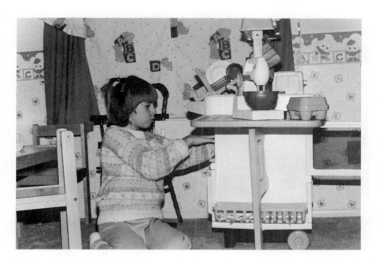

Figure 4-10 Nine years — MAKE-BELIEVE. Accident victim with mental impairment, though older in years — she enjoys playing in the toy kitchen that belongs to her tutor's child, with whom she plays often.

GAMES-WITH-RULES — (Child from car accident) — Here she plays a game-with-rules with her private tutor. This nine-year-old child has a much younger mental age, but she has accomplished a great many things — and enjoys playing! (Figure 4-11.)

Elements of Play

To review, the elements of play further the development of personality with special importance placed on fostering positive self-esteem. Observing these elements of play with exceptional children and their parents/teachers has been very rewarding. I have particularly come to appreciate the personalities of several of my severely handicapped friends (who happen to be children). When I began looking at them as "interesting personalities," my attitudes started changing for the better — and I have always thought my attitudes were very positive!

RESEARCH — This six-year-old boy was born with a condition that caused contractures (congenital malformations) of his limbs. He and his family have been involved with Crippled Children's Services since he was a very young child. Two pictures are shown here because he told me he wanted to show me "all the things I can do with these plastic balls." Intriguing play to watch! Also note his look of positive self-identity! He attends a regular first grade. (Figure 4-12 and Figure 4-13.)

OCCUPATIONAL THERAPY — The car accident victim has time for spontaneous play in the pool after her physical therapy. She enjoys the play; it particularly relieves her

Figure 4-11   Nine years — GAMES-WITH-RULES. Here the accident victim plays a simple game with her tutor.

Figure 4-12   Six years — RESEARCH. The child still has challenges with his limbs, but is mainstreamed in a regular schoolroom and can do almost everything — including most types of play.

Figure 4-13   Six years — RESEARCH PLAY. You can see his leg brace as he kicks. The entire family has helped with his problems.

Figure 4-14   Two and nine years — OCCUPATIONAL THERAPY. After a long day of school and after-school therapies, the accident victim is glad to be in the swimming pool. All her stress seems to float away as she plays with a teacher and her child.

stress after a long day. She also enjoys the socialization with her therapist's daughter. (Figure 4-14.)

I am "officially handicapped" as I have been severely hearing impaired for many years. Since learning about the occupational therapy function of play, I have noticed that I sometimes play games with my speech-reading skills to relieve stress. I hope others might gain some insight into their own playful actions as they read this book. Many adults have told me that what they need is to learn how to be more playful in their own lives!

APPRENTICESHIP-TO-LIVING — A two-year-old has Down Syndrome. He likes to play with domestic objects and learns much about the world he lives in as he does so. His parents, siblings, and grandparents play with him, as do his teachers. Child is progressing rapidly.

RECREATION — This seven-year-old girl was born with a condition which caused an absence of three limbs and malformation of the other. (Figure 4-15.) She attended one of the regular nursery schools in our Child Labs where the teachers found that she had very good balance even though she had such special challenges. This has helped in her skill development. Lindsay attends a regular classroom now. She wears her protheses during the week, Figure 4-15, but says "it's so much nicer not to wear them on the weekend while I am at home." In Figure 4-16 she jumps rope! FUN!

Figure 4-15   Seven years — RECREATION. Child with physical challenges enjoys music activities at home. Note her positive personality — it shows.

Figure 4-16   Seven years — RECREATION. She enjoys jumping rope without her prostheses being on. She does very well and has fun, too.

Solitary	Exercise
Recreation	3P

Provisions for Play

This was the portion of her study of play that Dr. Mary Sheridan became very involved with during her forty years as a medical doctor. To review, Dr. Sheridan found that by observing children in naturalistic settings, she understood a great deal more about growth and development of the child than she had through traditional studying. She particularly gained information about children by observing their spontaneous play. This knowledge convinced her that the young, handicapped children she treated should have the same provisions for play that non-handicapped children have even though adaptations would need to be made. I agree with Dr. Sheridan and have found that much is being done; however, there is much more to be accomplished. Let's continue describing the pictures from the provisions for play as shown in the "Play: A Vehicle to Learn about Living" framework.

PLAYTHINGS — This eighteen-month-old boy had a stroke when he was four months old. He has received much help through a children's hospital as well as from his family. In our "respite lab" he enjoys playing with the regular playthings, placed so that he has to stretch. Even though one side of his body is affected, he adapts very well and plays with most of the toys that other children use. (Figure 4-17.)

PLAYTIME — Circle Time in a Child Development Center in a session for severely handicapped children. Even though each child has an aide (often a volunteer) during this part of the day, the group enjoys this time together; it's evident as one watches. The teacher leading this circle loves her work; that is also evident. Although most of each day

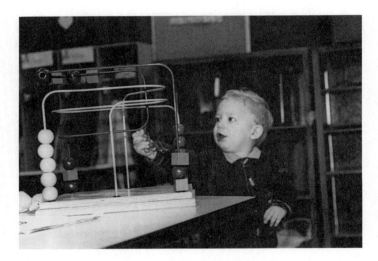

Figure 4-17   Eighteen months — PLAYTHINGS. Child had a stroke at four months. He plays with many "regular" toys which are placed so that he has to stretch. *(Courtesy of Health & Welfare Child Developmental Center, Region 7, Idaho)*

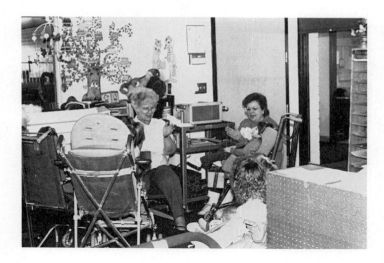

Figure 4-18   PLAYTIME. Children in a child development center enjoy circle time. Each of these severely handicapped children has an aide who helps the child take control of the play when possible. *(Courtesy of Health & Welfare Child Development Center, Region 7, Idaho)*

is spent in specific task development, there is time for this enjoyable interaction of adults and children. This skilled teacher looks for ways to give each child choices, too. (Figure 4-18.)

PLAYMATES — Lindsay, the child with missing limbs, is good on the trampoline, but she enjoys it so much more with her friends — the twins from across the street. They do gymnastic routines together — Lindsay on the trampoline, Figure 4-19, and the twins on the ground near the trampoline, Figure 4-20. Of course, sometimes they play on the trampoline together, Figure 4-21.

PLAYSPACE — This boy in a classroom within a Child Development Center has a special table for his play/work. Note the blackboard behind him. It extends clear to the floor so that children with all types of special needs can use the blackboard in their play. (Figure 4-22.)

READING BOOKS — Most handicapped children love books, too. This child with multiple challenges is enjoying the companionate play with her teacher/trainer in the "respite lab." (Figure 4-23.)

Figure 4-19   PLAYMATES. Lindsay is very good on the trampoline, but she enjoys it more with her friends, the twins from across the street.

Figure 4-20   Seven years — PLAYMATES. Here the twins are doing their gymnastic routines near Lindsay's trampoline. Fun!

Figure 4-21   Seven years — PLAYMATES. Here Lindsay does routines on the trampoline with one of the twins.

Figure 4-22   Five years — PLAYSPACE. This child is able to interact and play with others because the space has been adapted to suit his needs. *(Courtesy of Health & Welfare Child Developmental Center, Region 7, Idaho)*

Figure 4-23   Five years — This child has multiple challenges, but enjoys having a teacher read to her. Here they are singing a song that goes with the story. *(Courtesy of Ricks College Respite Labs)*

Companionate	M.B. (Perhaps)
Recreation	4P

PLAY CAN BE A "VEHICLE FOR LEARNING ABOUT LIVING" FOR HANDICAPPED CHILDREN, TOO

So what do the pictures and the descriptions of the children in the pictures above tell us? INSOFAR AS POSSIBLE, THE IMPAIRED/HANDICAPPED CHILD NEEDS TO HAVE THE SAME OPPORTUNITIES TO PLAY AS ANY CHILD DOES. Let's review the list of some of the main things a child does in play:

- experiments with people and things
- develops positive self-esteem and self-respect
- stores his memory
- studies causes and effects
- reasons out problems
- builds up a useful vocabulary
- learns to control his self-centered emotional reactions
- develops fine and gross motor skills
- adapts his behavior to the cultural habits of his social group.

Of course, there would need to be some adaptations to this list for children with special needs. For one child the list might include: studies causes and effects with toys that have been designed or adapted especially for children with his impairment. For another it might say: develops the fine and gross motor skills of her upper body so that she can participate in more activities from her wheelchair or on the mats, etc.

We can also expand an earlier quote and say, "Play is as necessary to an exceptional child's development of body, intellect, and personality as are food, shelter, fresh air, exercise, rest, and the prevention of illness and accidents. The young child is entitled to play; it is *each* child's heritage!"

PLAYTHINGS AND PLAY EQUIPMENT

The essential provisions for play were identified as playthings, playspace, playtime, and playmates. These same provisions are essential for special needs children, too. It is interesting to note that much of the extensive research of the past decade has confirmed what Dr. Sheridan said after her forty years of working with handicapped children:

> Hence, from long experience, I would stress my conviction that all the well-tried traditional playthings such as rattles, balls, blocks, dolls, wheeled toys and everyday household objects, from which normal children derive so much pleasure and profit, are of primary and not secondary importance in the natural, happy, fundamental learning of handicapped children.

Many toys can be adapted for children with special needs. Switches that turn off and on by various methods (lightly touching, blowing, etc.) enable many handi-capable children to enjoy play activities. Cassette players can be adapted in many different ways and the child can control the starting and stopping of the cassette so that he is very involved and has control of the playing of the tapes.

There are excellent books and other resources available. Many college and city libraries have special sections for those who have impairments and those who work with the handicapped. Often the librarians in these sections are great resource persons. The larger or more innovative libraries often have Toy Lending Libraries. Regular and adaptive toys can be checked out to utilize with a child. Often being able to use a toy will give ideas of ways to adapt the plaything so that it will suit the needs of a particular child better. Information about adaptive equipment and playthings can also be gained from studying the excellent catalogs that are available today. One does need knowledge concerning the development of the child, though, because some of the catalogs extend the use of the equipment/playthings they are trying to sell. (Remember the listing of toys in appendix B.)

Figures 4-24 and 4-25 show Jason, a child born with cerebral palsy. This child, now five, speaks little although he communicates with gestures, eye contact, etc. Jason and his parents have been to special commercial workshops given by companies in order to try out equipment that might be best suited for him. (An example is that he has a special device, commercially made, that allows him to do many playful actions in a swimming pool.) But many of his playthings have been adapted by his innovative parents. A "switch plate" saved from his last wheelchair allows him to play with remote-control toys similar

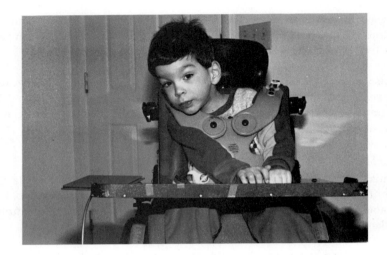

Figure 4-24   Five years — Jason is learning to use special adaptive switches to play with a remote-control car like his brother and other friends do. *(Courtesy of Pugmire Photography)*

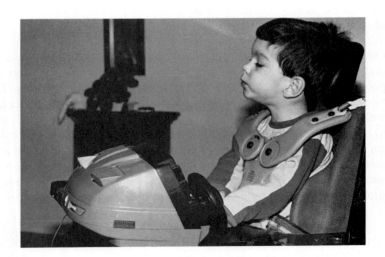

Figure 4-25   Five years — Jason also has a steering wheel toy that has been adapted for his use. Note his look of self-esteem. He can control the play! *(Courtesy of Pugmire Photography)*

to the way that other children do, Figure 4-24. Note his look of self-identity as he controls his own play, Figure 4-25. At Christmas time, his mother rigged up lights on his wheelchair that he could turn off and on with a special switch. He really liked the effects he could create with the switch and enjoyed the attention he gained from others around him as they watched him play.

Playspace

Playspaces for children with all types of handicaps are being designed and built; those working with handicapped children are learning to use them. Often this means, "HANDS OFF, TEACHERS/PARENTS! THESE PLACES ARE SAFE. LET THESE CHILDREN CONTROL THEIR OWN ACTIONS AND TRULY *PLAY*!" Granted such playgrounds and indoor play spaces are not as numerous as we would wish, but there is progress being made. These playspaces are found in homes as well as child centers, hospitals, and communities.

The same comment already made regarding the needs of normal children for a "personal territory" applies with equal pertinence to handicapped children. Indoor playroooms must be clean, warm, and safe as well as suitably equipped. Although, as stated above, special playgrounds for children with all kinds of handicaps are desirable, the use of common outdoor playground equipment should be encouraged provided reasonable safety precautions are taken and adequate supervision is available. Handicapped children of all ages enjoy active play that is within their physical capacities. They should therefore be given suitable opportunities for play with trucks, tricycles, pedal cars, climbing apparatus, slides, teeter-totters and sandpiles. Their sensible use promotes mobility, self-reliance, and good companionship.

Playtime

ADEQUATE TIME FOR EACH CHILD TO PLAY! This is one of the main pleas of this book and includes a plea that each child with special needs will have time to play spontaneously, too. Sometimes these children are so busy with therapies of various types that they have little time for activities over which they have inner control and free choice. Granted, some handicapped children may never progress to the point of using inner control, but many do and could well use more of their time in true play. Play that promotes social skills and helps the children build friendships is especially desirable. It is well known among those who actually work with exceptional children that even children who are severely impaired by certain conditions enjoy the association of other people and a feeling of being in a group. An added problem for many handicapped children (mentioned above in reference to Hannah) is that they become social isolates in their own neighborhoods or community settings because they have not had the time to learn the give and take and the joy that comes from peer play. Studies have shown that integration between handicapped and nonhandicapped children will require special efforts (Odom, Jenkins, Speltz and DeKlyen 1982). More needs to be done with this problem, but the task is being faced.

Many special-needs children are able to take part in various outdoor activities because of efforts by certain groups of people. The Special Olympics are probably the best known of these programs and children with many types of impairments take part in various athletic events. Preparation for Winter Special Olympics finds many handi-capable children on the ski slopes with volunteers who find meaning in their lives by helping these young people. In other places volunteers are building special facilities that enable handicapped children to be involved in horseback riding. Being involved with horses has helped many types of exceptional children. Particular succes has been shown with autistic children (Williams 1990).

Some mentally impaired children will only progress to an infant or toddler level of play. But even nonhandicapped infants and toddlers enjoy the pleasure of human interaction and play; so will the majority of these mentally challenged children.

An example is a study that shows that four-year-old Down Syndrome children with a mental age of two play in ways that toddlers do (Switzky, Ludwig and Haywood 1979).

Figure 4-26 shows Hannah, my friend with William's Syndrome, and me in her classroom. After we took pictures, Hannah said, "There's some time to play. Let's do a puzzle!" She knew what playthings could be used, where they were located, and that she was free to control her own playing as her school tasks were done.

Figure 4-26   Nine years — Hannah, the William's Syndrome child, uses her play time to do a puzzle. She was delighted to have her friend (your author) do the puzzle with her.

Figure 4-27   Child in center is severely hearing impaired, but he is "one of the kids" as he plays in a regular preschool group. *(Courtesy of Ricks College Respite Labs)*

Playmates

As with nonhandicapped children, the child's first playmates are usually her parents, particularly the mother. This is good for both child and parent as play gives them a chance to learn more about each other. Later, siblings become playmates, but often these children have to be taught ways to play with their brothers or sisters. This is why the Individualized Family Service Plans (IFSP) being implemented by the provisions of PL 99–457 show such promise. When the family as a whole is strong, the individual members show more capabilities to handle their challenges in life.

Some comments have already been made about the risk of the handicapped becoming social isolates. With children being mainstreamed earlier in Head Start and various types of nursery groups, it is hopeful that this will not happen as often. Figure 4-27 shows a child in one of our regular nursery groups who is severely hearing impaired. The three children are playing with a wooden-roller tracking toy (for marbles). The marble is rolled down the wooden frame and is caught in various kinds of containers that cause different sounds to be made. As the reader can tell, this handi-capable child is "one of the kids" playing spontaneously and learning about living with the other children.

PLAY WITHIN SOME SPECIAL NEEDS GROUPS

There are many types of special-needs groups although in most cases each child with special challenges is regarded as an individual as his educational program or services plan is developed. However, the play needs of the various types of exceptional children can be discussed from the standpoint of groups. Practical suggestions will be given so that people preparing to facilitate the play of the individual exceptional child can help that child learn more about living!

Children from Birth to Three

PL 99–457 does not require that children from birth to three be labelled as having a specific developmental impairment or delay in order to get educational funding. Simply put, this means that a child does not have to be called mentally retarded or emotionally disturbed, etc. These youngest children are so individual in their development. Those of us who have long been interested in these children have pled not to have "limiting labels pasted on the child so soon." Rather, we would like to observe and use the knowledge that has been gained about child development so that each child can be helped in the best way possible.

Play is the natural activity for almost every child. Valuable information can be gained about ways to help the individual as he is observed playing. The possibilities of learning about the youngest through their spontaneous play is a potentiality that must not be overlooked. And, of course, play can help the child with special needs learn to socialize with others and develop his personality and mind, too.

An example of this is two-year-old Joanna who is in our regular toddler program. Joanna has an impairment that affects one side of her body as well as her language development. She is receiving the help of a speech therapist, a physical therapist, and an occupational therapist. The workers in our labs follow the suggestions of these therapists and her mother, but are pleased that this team wants Joanna to have spontaneous play experiences within a structured environment that will help with her particular challenges. Recently we videotaped Joanna during an entire lab session. We were surprised as we noted the many and varied types and functions of play that Joanna used. Socially speaking, we had thought she basically was involved in solitary play, but there was parallel, associative, and even a moment of truly cooperative play! Gross motor development came as Joanna crawled through the cloth tunnel-tube several times; she used both sides of her body as she crawled. In our outdoor playground, Joanna wanted to climb on the rocks. She was carefully supervised, of course, but the joy of her spontaneous play on the rocks made her stretch and reach repeatedly. Fine motor skills were developed as she used several of the art media such as painting at the easel and using play dough. Intellectual challenges were met as she played games involving big pictures of items in her own environment, such as familiar animals. Problem solving was used in several simple dramatic play incidents, especially "ironing" in the housekeeping area. However, it was the language development that was most exciting to the teachers. Joanna decided to use and resuse the word "orange." (She had not used this word before in the lab.) She spontaneously created her own game saying the word "orange" and finding orange items in the lab. With new

Figure 4-28 Two-and-a-half years — Severely hearing impaired, along with other problems, he has just made the sign for Mama and uttered "Mama"! He gets a loving hug from his foster mother, who also operates a day care center in her home. *(Courtesy of Walton Foster and Day*

opportunities in group situations and therapists who have suggested individualized ways for Joanna to be helped, she has the prospect of leading a richer, fuller life than she would have just a few years ago. Her family, teachers, and therapists work together to bring this about.

Another child whom we shall call "Child J" is shown in a series of pictures taken in a foster home setting, Figure 4-28 through Figure 4-31. "J" has multiple impairments, but his foster parents do not apply labels to him. They enourage and praise him and the results are extra-ordinary. (Granted it has taken over two years of concentrated loving, skilled care to accomplish this). As the reader can see in the pictures, "J" decides he will go to the sandpile as his friend is doing. He heads out, crawling, over the textured sidewalk. (This gives him additional sensory stimulation as well as gross motor experience.) He arrives at the protected sandpile that has slats around it to encourage the non-standers to pull themselves up if they wish. He joins in the associative play. It could be called apprenticeship-to-living as he learns to interact with others more effectively. But, oh, to see his look of accomplishment. And the choice to go to the sandpile was his!

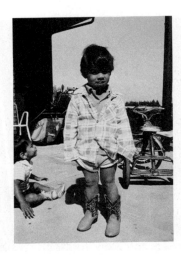

Figure 4-29   Two-and-a-half and four years — This "regular" child in the day care home sets the example. He is admired and imitated with children with challenges. *(Courtesy of Walton Foster and Day Care Home, Idaho Falls, Idaho)*

Figure 4-30   Two-and-a-half years — "You can do it!" suggests the "regular" child (using gestures for communication). So off to the sand box goes this two-and-a-half year old. *(Courtesy of Walton Foster and Day Care Home, Idaho Falls, Idaho)*

Figure 4-31   Two-and-a-half years — Crawling over textured, but safe, materials helps him in many ways. Members of the foster family watch closely but let him experience success. *(Courtesy of Walton Foster and Day Care Home, Idaho Falls, Idaho)*

PLAY AMONG CHILDREN WITH SPECIFIC IMPAIRMENTS

Perhaps the time will come when children are not "grouped" according to their disability or impairment. Special-needs children could be called by their curriculum emphasis. Just as a college student is referred to as an English major, a child could be referred to as language emphasis student. However, for the present, referring to children by their general impairment is a common practice; we use the terms just as a basis for discussing some of the play needs of groups of children.

Children Who Are Physically Challenged

This is a large group with exceedingly variable conditions, some of which have existed from birth while others have been acquired as a result of disease or injury. Some serious disablements are the result of conditions such as cerebral palsy; others are malformations of the arms, hands, legs, or feet. Some result from accidents at home, in the street, or in vehicles. The causes are multitudinous, but the challenge is that each child represents his unique problems for pediatricians, therapists, bio-engineers, and teachers. Consequently, early home management and later educational placement require very careful consideration. Physically impaired children are often such rewarding pupils that there may be a danger that they will be pressured too much and allowed too little opportunity for relaxation and simple fun.

APPLICATION FOR CAREGIVERS

The basic principles for guiding a child to play are followed in the examples above — with adaptations:

1. The caregivers *OBSERVE* the child's actions and *LISTEN* to language. Lack of these attributes are noted as well as the child's strengths. Each caregiver is aware of the development, interests, and needs of the child and they work together, Figure 4-32.
2. *CREATE PROVISIONS FOR PLAY* (toys, space, and setups that encourage play with friends) for each child in the group, but particularly with the impaired child's special needs in mind, Figure 4-33.
3. The caregivers are aware of play being a vehicle for each child to learn about living more effectively. Play setups especially *ENCOURAGE SPONTANEOUS PLAY*. Each caregiver looks for opportunities to build positive self-identity and attitudes as well as needed skills. Sometimes other children can be the one to build positive self-identity in the child, too, Figure 4-34.
4. The child's "plan" will be reviewed and ways to help her/him move to the next step of the short-term goals will be determined. The caregivers will often *HELP THE CHILD FOCUS* on the new toy or play setup if that child needs encouragement and is ready to move to the next level of play, Figure 4-35.
5. The caregiver *LETS THE CHILD TAKE CONTROL OF THE PLAY* as much as possible. With the handi-capable child this may involve adaptations of toys, environment, etc., Figure 4-36.

Children with mobility defects often cannot explore for themselves nor follow adults around the house and learn to imitate their everyday activities. Moreover, for many children with cerebral palsy and head injuries, normal integration and interpretation of sensory experience, which depend not only upon intake, but also upon memory storage, may be disturbed. In these circumstances, initiation of premotor assembly, i.e., sequential forward 'programming' of voluntary movements, is likely to present serious difficulty. Appropriate provisions for play can often be made more effectively by using information gained from observational experience.

Some children with severe physical handicaps receive special training both at home and at centers if their disabilities are of the nature that can be helped at both places. By the time they are old enough for regular play groups, preschools, or kindergarten they can cope quite well in the regular classroom for the main part of the day. Sometimes special equipment must be obtained or adjustments made to the school facilities.

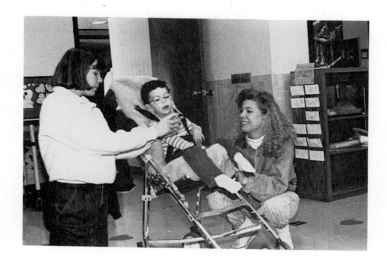

Figure 4-32 First — OBSERVE and LISTEN to the child and the principal caregiver. This mom knows what her child needs and wants. *(Courtesy of Ricks College Respite Labs)*

Figure 4-33 Second — PROVIDE SUITABLE PROVISIONS for play. This three-year-old child with cerebral palsy loves to "gently" play the piano. *(Courtesy of Ricks College Respite Labs)*

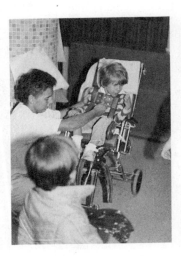

Figure 4-34 Third — ENCOURAGE spontaneous play. A student teacher helps a blind girl. The boy in the foreground would like to play. The teacher looks for ways to bring this about. (*Courtesy of Ricks College Respite Labs*)

Figure 4-35 Fourth — FOCUS. This teacher is skilled in her ability to help children who have difficulty focusing their attention. There are times for work and play in her classroom.

Figure 4-36   Fifth — Let the child TAKE CONTROL of the play. Mom is there to encourage and help Jason focus on the game, but he controls the play. *(Courtesy of Ricks College Respite Labs)*

It is a valuable learning experience to watch the adaptive behaviors of some of these physically impaired youngsters and to note the many things their parents and caseworkers have done to help them live as fully as possible. An example is Randy whom you met in the Framework of Play above. Randy was six-years-old when Figures 4-13 and 4-14 were taken. He was born with arthrogryposis (congenital contractures, malformation of the limbs). This child not only had early and vigorous physical therapy combined with proper orthopedic and surgical intervention, but his family members encouraged him in each way that was suggested by his caseworkers and medical personnel, Figure 4-37. They also used their own insights and observed his interests in order to see what kind of play he needed. He enjoyed playing games with family members and wanted to be part of their activities. So they found toys and other playthings or made them so that he could join in the play and active/exercise play by himself. Now he is able to take part in many games requiring motor skills that he might not have been able to do without their encouragement. His personality is pleasant and he is excited to show his expertise with balls, Figure 4-38.

Marsha Johnson, the teacher of the preschool referred to in this chapter, has had cerebral palsy since she was born. At that time (the 1950s) there was not the help available that there is now. Marsha's parents were determined that she would be as much a part of the regular world as possible. Her father fixed the animal pen so that Marsha had to stretch in order to do her work — feeding the calf its bottle. (There is not a clear picture available of this, but Figure 4-39 illustrates it.) Marsha remembers her feelings of achievement and happiness at this involvement in the family's business. Now we would call it the child's "positive self-esteem." She enjoyed these types of activities better than playing with toys.

Figure 4-37   Three-and-a-half years — Randy spent a lot of time in doctors' offices. Here he plays with a miniature toy. His family played with him regularly at home. *(Courtesy of Health & Welfare Child Developmental Center, Region 7, Idaho)*

Figure 4-38   Six years — Now Randy can play so many games. He is in a regular first grade and part of a family that really plays together.

Figure 4-39 Marsha was born with cerebral palsy in the 1950s. Her father made arrangements for her to feed the calf. This was her work and her play; it helped her self-esteem. *(Courtesy of Jenny Moser-Anderson, Illustrator)*

Solitary	Practice/Exercise
Occ. Therapy	3P

Her work and play were literally the same activity. An excellent and recognized preschool teacher now, Figure 4-40, Marsha often uses this principle of finding activities that build self-esteem as she plans for her students' work and play. She is especially aware of the opportunities for spontaneous play, e.g., having a new substance such as rice in the sandtable and many devices for the children to use for measuring and pouring.

Mental Retardation

These children constitute a large and a most diverse group of children with impairments/handicaps. They present every variety and degree of retarded development. Many have additional defects of vision and hearing which add to their intellectual difficulties. Only a few years ago, these additional difficulties often went unnoticed. Now, the great majority of these children have comprehensive pediatric assessments. As stated previously, it is hoped that PL 99–457 will help even more with this identification of challenges as these children receive help at an earlier age.

Children with Down Syndrome form a major subgroup. They often show general delay in all aspects of development, particularly in language acquisition. With newer techniques of working with these children, though, more and more are gaining competence in skills and abilities that were considered beyond them even a few years ago. Down Syndrome children are often affectionate, contented, and socially acceptable little children, Figure 4-41. In their play they are notably imitative and this allows them to be helped in many

Figure 4-40   Marsha, the teacher, is now a recognized early childhood specialist. She selects activities for students that help them build positive self-esteem. *(Courtesy of Joe Hamilton State Preschool, Crescent City, California)*

Companionate	M.B. (later)
App. to Living	4P

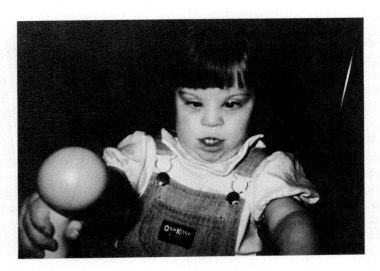

Figure 4-41   Two-and-a-half years — Down Syndrome child plays contentedly. Loved by family and day care workers, this child has a pleasant personality. *(Courtesy of Health & Welfare Child Developmental Center, Region 7, Idaho)*

Solitary	Pr./Ex.
Research Fun	3P

ways. They usually benefit greatly from amiable, skilled training, teaching, and supervision.

One study (Gibbs and Carswell 1988) that may be considered representative of newer techniques being used showed how Total Communication (using sign language with oral language) was used with a fourteen-month-old prelinguistic Down Syndrome child. A play-based language intervention was designed. As the abstract to the study says, "Two equivalent ten-word sets were introduced during free play; with one set of ten toys, manual signs augmented speech, while for the other ten toys only speech was used. Results indicated that comprehension was not differentially affected by the type of communication approach used. However, the child was able to use manual signs expressively many months before any understandable words were used. His use of manual signs did not inhibit his use of speech (EDRS Document 296 542). (An example of how this was used in a spontaneous play situation is given later.)

A group that causes special concern are the children that were born far too early. Although neonatal intensive care units have enabled many of these babies to survive and live normal lives, other children often have severe handicaps including differing degrees of intellectual impairment. Often a mother who has had difficulty with a previous pregnancy will get help from regional health clinics during a subsequent pregnancy. Babies with other types of problems are seen at these clinics, of course. Some of the illustrations in this book have been taken at these maternity and infant or "infants-at-risk" clinics, Figure 4-42 and 4-43. I have been impressed with the dedication of various types of workers who have exhibited great skill as they worked with these children and their parents. Some of

Figure 4-42 At the maternity and infant clinic. A father waits with baby while mother is seeing a doctor. Photographer just missed interactive spontaneous play between Dad and child. (*Courtesy of Health & Welfare Child Developmental Center, Region 7, Idaho*)

Figure 4-43   Eleven months — Child sits competently exploring his diaper bag while his mother waits for a doctor's appointment to find out if the child has developmental delays. *(Courtesy of Health & Welfare Child Developmental Center, Region 7, Idaho)*

Solitary	Pr./Ex.
Occ. Therapy	4P

these parents do not know how to use effective companionate play with their children and workers teach them how to do this.

Children in Hospitals or with Temporary Special Needs

A child in a hospital or with a temporary challenge has a very special need of playthings and playmates appropriate to his age and disability as well as to the unusual environmental circumstances, Figure 4-44 through Figure 4-46. Although it is unwise to overcrowd his bed with too many toys as this tends to confuse him, he needs to have more than one at a time available if he is not to become bored. If he is at the stage of throwing things out of his crib, he may use the skill frequently in order to attract adult attention or to seek cooperation in give-and-take play. Various hospitals have ways of handling this; some firmly tie the throwable playthings to the crib making certain that this is done in a safe manner.

Older children dislike to think that they have fallen behind their classmates when they return to school. Indeed, for most children of school age, once they have recovered from the acute phases of an illness or operation, lessons are the most welcome form of occupational therapy. Hence the hospital playroom personnel and/or the child's teacher/tutor are indispensable members of staff in children's wards.

Figure 4-44   Four months — Beautiful wide-eyed baby, with a broken leg.

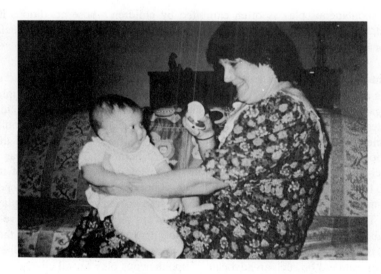

Figure 4-45   Four months — Mom plays with baby in previous picture. Mom demonstrates the "give-and-take" Dr. Sheridan recommended for the temporarily handicapped child.

Companionate	Pr./Ex.
Occ. Therapy	4P

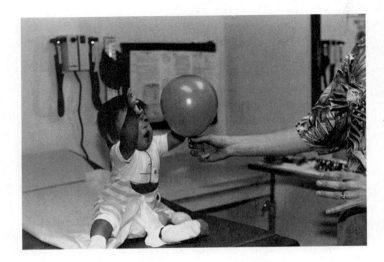

Figure 4-46   Eight months — Child being adopted must have a special skin test. His playmate is the pediatric nurse. *(Courtesy of Health & Welfare Child Developmental Center, Region 7, Idaho)*

Creative, spontaneous play is often exhibited by children whose conditions have been diagnosed, but who have to spend long hours in clinic waiting rooms for checkups from specialists and/or case workers.

Pictured in Figure 4-47 is a nine-year-old girl who was waiting to see a noted specialist. There was a "preschool-testing" eye chart on the wall of the clinic. This delightful child made up games with the chart which she played by herself. First she was the child having her eyes tested and then she became the person giving the eye test. (We would call the basic element of her play "occupational therapy: relief from boredom" and the type of play "sociodramatic: pretending to take the role of another.") The author was delighted with the chance to observe this spontaneous play. Having become aware of it, she has since seen this in many younger and handicapped children, too. Granted their spontaneous play is simpler and shorter in duration, but it is some of the most creative play she has observed. The waiting parents or guardians are always pleased when a positive comment is made about their child and they have reported that once they looked for that type of creativity, they recognized it often. This is an example, also, of the way Dr. Sheridan, the pediatrician, came to be such an advocate of spontaneous play for all children, especially the handicapped.

Some children are temporarily handicapped because of an injury or illness, but they are able to recuperate just fine at home. Often, parents will consult local centers or persons whom they know are trained in guiding the play of children with special needs to gain advice for helping their own child during the time of the child's disability.

Figure 4-47   Nine years — Delightful older child with special challenge uses solitary pretense play to relieve the boredom, while waiting for a noted specialist at a clinic. Note kindergarten eye chart on the wall. *(Courtesy of Health & Welfare Child Developmental Center, Region 7, Idaho)*

Visually Impaired Children

This is a numerically small but seriously impaired group. Visual disorders arise from a multitude of causes either within the eye itself or in those areas of the brain that deal with the interpretation of visual phenomena. Lacking normal opportunities to relate visually to their caregivers, they must learn from attentive listening, and from smelling, touching, and manipulating whatever exists within arm's reach. They generally dislike soft toys, and need playthings that provide good "feelable" shapes and textures and above all a meaningful language. It is comparatively easy for sighted people to shut their own eyes in order to appreciate the grievous deprivations of total blindness. But it is more difficult to understand the baffling visual world of a partially sighted child who may possess some "patches" of comparatively useful near vision, but who has little notion of distances and perspectives of spatial relationships, and therefore cannot readily appreciate our predominantly visually organized world.

Blind children are easily distracted by sound. If background noise is too prominent they cannot focus attention on meaningful elements in the environment for long, and so, in self-defense, tend to drift into a state of non-attention, often engaging in the "blindisms" merely in order to keep themselves in contact with reality. Blindisms may include flipping their hand back and forth (as in Figure 4-48), poking their fingers into their eyes, making strange noises, rocking back and forth, and spinning around. These mannerisms are inappropriate and parents/caregivers need to help the child replace them by leading them to more appropriate activities. Playspaces (environments) and playthings are very important,

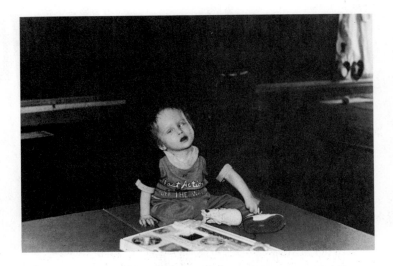

Figure 4-48   Three years — Totally blind child is using a "self stim" (blindism) with his left hand. He appeared to respond to the flash of the camera. *(Courtesy of Health & Welfare Child Developmental Center, Region 7, Idaho)*

Solitary	Pr./Ex.
App. to Living, Fun	3P

Figure 4-49. When the blind or severely visually impaired child has room to move about safely, she gains confidence and more quickly learns the skill of moving through a familiar space.

Young blind children, unable to see how both hands function together, may be unaware of how to bring this about. Even when bilateral function is explained and illustrated, they may still need to feel the position of one hand with the other. If, in addition, they have a central (cortical) spatial difficulty, their learning problems are indescribably complex.

The little girl pictured in Figure 4-50 was mainstreamed in a preschool class in an exemplary center. As I was taking pictures, this blind child was so involved in the spontaneous, associative play going on with the other children that it was easy to understand why the term "handi-capable" is being used more widely. I returned to observe her when she started kindergarten. She was doing very well in her work and play activities.

Children with Seriously Impaired Hearing

Such children must come to terms with people and learn about the world in which they live mainly through looking, touching, smelling, and exploring their environment visually; they must communicate with other people in any way open to them. Most deaf children do have some hearing; this is called "residual." It is essential that every method possible be used to utilize this. Therefore they should be encouraged as very young children to employ every available avenue of human communication, including facial

Figure 4-49 Three years — Blind child has overcome his tactile defensiveness and is responding to the toy. Skilled, devoted professionals have helped him achieve this milestone. *(Courtesy of Health & Welfare Child Developmental Center, Region 7, Idaho)*

Figure 4-50 While taking this picture, the photographer did not realize that the child in the center was blind. She played right along with the others. *(Courtesy of Health & Welfare Child Developmental Center, Region 7, Idaho)*

expressions, meaningful gestures, pictures, and drawings. Many hearing-impaired children communicate during play by using representative toys (both child-sized and miniatures) of people, animals, domestic items, transportation objects, etc.

Most children with any residual hearing wear some type of hearing aid, but there are differing opinions on how early this should be done. As I have been severely hearing impaired since a fairly young age, I have been impressed that most very young children adapt to their hearing aids very quickly. These children recognize that the amplified hearing opens new avenues of communication to them. Learning from parents in the waiting rooms of doctors, audiologists, and speechreading teachers, I have been excited by the fact that hearing-impaired children are now given many different types of experiences in order to gain the best total communication that each one is capable of developing. For many children this includes sign language. It is interesting to note that children who learn sign as their primary language go through the same state of acquiring language as do children in any language or in any culture. They first learn single signs and as the signs are combined, they overgeneralize. Then they learn to sign using more complete thoughts.

As is the case when working with many handicapping conditions, field workers and parents have had to learn about the best kinds of play as they guided the progress of a specific child, Figure 4-51 through Figure 4-53. This is especially true of very young handicapped children. Often hospitals or clinics have developed practical and worthwhile ideas that they pass on to others. An example is the "Parent-Infant Curriculum: Hometraining for Parents and Hearing Impaired Infants 0-4 Years" from the Good Samaritan Hospital and Medical Center in Portland, Oregon. Playful activities, such as

Figure 4-51 Four years — Surgery has improved Katie's hearing ability. She wears hearing aids, but has language delays.

Solitary	Constructive
App. to Living	4P

Figure 4-52 Teacher moves to help Katie. She gets Katie to answer questions like "What shall we build with these blocks?"

Companionate	Constructive
App. to Living	4P

Figure 4-53 Teacher encourages a nearby friend to join Katie. Soon the children have taken control and it evolves into delightful spontaneous play.

Associative	M.B.
App. to Living	4P

finding an alarm clock when it goes off (for twelve-months and older child), are described along with the objectives for the activity. I would call many of these exercises "apprecticeship-to-living," but I admire the way they are presented in a context of play. The child often has control over much of the action. It is suggested that the older child with some residual hearing play games that compare environmental sounds. Most of these games are enjoyed by nonhandicapped children, too. In fact, many of the activities could be called recreation.

Children with Other Disorders of Communication

These children present numerous widely-differing and sometimes very serious problems requiring multiprofessional assessment and therapy. The causes of their delayed linguistic development range from lack of normal opportunity to learn, to obscure central brain defects affecting reception, interpretation, or expression of language (Sheridan 1976).

Some children, especially those whose spontaneous use of ordinary playthings provides evidence of good understanding of the everyday world, readily respond to therapeutic intervention. Others, for instance many autistic children, who do not possess any effectual communication code, appear unable to construct mental blueprints for purposeful movements, although they possess all the necessary neuro-muscular equipment, Figure 4-54.

Whatever the cause or degree of linguistic disability, it is important to provide opportunities for spontaneous imitative and later inventive play. Play that necessitates being involved in personal relationships and the use of everyday objects is particularly important. Those involved in these personal relationships with the child can give strong positive

Figure 4-54   Three-and-a-half years — Autistic child with severe challenges. Arching of the back may be self-stimulating for this child. He does like to be outdoors. *(Courtesy of Walton Foster and Day Care Home, Idaho Falls, Idaho)*

Some play activities of two-year-old Joanna who has a serious language delay were listed earlier in this section. Joanna is in our Toddler Group; she is involved in a Total Communication plan similar to the one described previously (Gibbs and Carswell 1988), to help with the development of language skills, Figure 4-55. The information from the study above is a help to her caregivers. It gives ideas of ways to structure her play environment. We feel that we can say, "In addition to understanding developmental milestones and using astute observing, we can help a child through spontaneous play and by studying the available research." I also should add that we always keep the recreational element of the play framework in mind. Children are entitled to have FUN as they play!

(Note: I might add that the professor has fun, too. In a lab, our Joanna made the sign and said the word "Grandma" to me. I do know her grandmother so whether she meant me or her own grandmother, I could not tell, but I was delighted to take part in this child's progress and I joined her briefly in spontaneous play with the cornmeal in the big steel bowl.)

encouragement and can find ways to help him/her communicate in single words, meaningful vocalizations, and telling gestures.

Children with Severe Handicaps

Dr. Sheridan felt that some of the more bizarre manifestations of grossly abnormal motor, sensory, emotional, or social development such as apparently purposeless hyperactivity, inability to communicate, catastrophic tantrums, autistic withdrawal, and the like, can become less bewildering (and hopefully more accessible to therapy) if we regard the afflicted children as helplessly trapped in one of the earlier phases of development. Dr. Sheridan also thought concerned persons could argue that a particular handicapped child is overreacting to unintegrated perceptual inflow, or showing exploratory insatiability, compulsive clinging to transitional objects, inability to establish an effective code of communication, or that his social nonconformity is founded in some deep emotional stress.

There is some disagreement among educators/caregivers on the definition and/or characteristics of the severely handicapped child. Very often such a child has complex combinations of disabilities. What a child can do (not what he can't), how he manages to do it, and most importantly of all, whether he can be helped to do it more effectively are what really matter. Hopefully, finding the right plan for the individual child's particular challenges is the aim of all concerned. The day-to-day problems of parents of handicapped children have much more in common than in their differences. The parents' advisers need to possess more virtues than compassion and adequate financing, although both would surely be of a great help, particularly the latter! Workers in this field must be able to tell the painful truth when parental overoptimism regarding progress is even more unwarranted than overpessimism. After all, their child is handicapped and for many years will

Figure 4-55   Two-and-a-half years — Joanna was not talking when she entered our toddler lab. Her speech therapist is using sign to help with her verbal skills. It is working. Joanna is making the sign for "baby" and saying it. *(Courtesy of Ricks College, Toddler Lab)*

continue to need affection, patient encouragement, and sensible discipline, subject neither to overprotection nor to intolerable strain. It is hoped that each severely handicapped child will have pleasurable activities in his/her life, too, Figure 4-56.

PARENT SUPPORT GROUPS

The most frequent comment that I have heard from parents who have given their time and cooperation to make this book and its illustrations a reality, is that there is such a great turnover of workers. Often the parents feel they are training the caseworkers instead of being trained by them. However, great strides have been accomplished in the past few years. Parent support groups are a big factor in this progress.

The Idaho parents' asssociation has a great name — IPUL (*I*daho *P*arents [Professionals] *U*n*L*imited). Members live the philosophy "*I PULL FOR THE INDIVIDUAL HAND-ICAPPED CHILD!*" and endeavor to help others gain this philosophy. Parents meet to exchange ideas as well as understanding of agencies, rights, obligations, etc. When a new law or policy is being implemented, workshops are held to aid the parents. Workshops are also held on subjects of interest such as "Spontaneous Play — A Heritage for *each* child!" Professionals and students are invited if they wish to come to meetings, but the emphasis is for and by the parents. The Idaho Association has an office in our capitol; most state associations do. Because Idaho is basically a rural state, though, workshops are taken to the various regions so that all parents and professionals have opportunities to attend. An

Figure 4-56 The child on the right in the wheelchair (in a foster home) is five years old, but does nothing for herself. Although her head is down, she seems to like being with the other playing children. *(Courtesy of Walton Foster and Day Care Home, Idaho Falls, Idaho)*

excellent newsletter is sent to all interested parties. As mentioned previously, there are also support groups for many of the specific groups of persons with special needs.

...AND SO THE "VEHICLE OF PLAY" MOVES ON!

Little did I realize when I created my Vehicle of Play what a long and special "drive" lay ahead of me. Preparation for this book has taken me back to a previous generation to recall — and in some instances, study documented materials — when former students and dear friends were young children. I have had the privilege of studying their children and the chance to record data that shows basic similarities and differences of children from one generation to the next, Figure 4-57. I have travelled through several states and into scores of schools, agencies, libraries, research settings, playgrounds, etc. However, it has also taken me into homes that were only a few blocks from my main residence. In each of these places I have learned a great deal about children — both those who appear to have normal lives and those who have moderate to severe challenges. I have come to have GREAT respect for the spontaneous play of children. I have learned from these spontaneous players some of the best ways to live. Much of it can be summarized by referring to the *elements of play* that help the individual to gain further growth. I have gained a greater respect for the discovery, the observing, the exploring, and the speculating of *research play*. I have learned from studying the *occupational therapy* element of play to relax and be playful when I am full of stress and when I have pain. (I am fortunate; I am

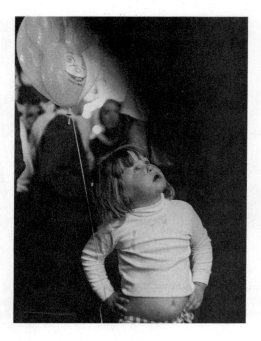

Figure 4-57   The Vehicle of Play Moves On....Here is Laurie — pausing in her play. She was a child with learning disabilities. Her parents were "ahead of their time" in the ways they helped her. There was always time for play. Now Laurie is the mother of the delightful child in Figure 2-10. *(Courtesy of Pugmire Photography)*

never bored.) I comprehend with more insight that one can always gain more competence in everyday living and a playful approach (called *apprenticeship-to-living*) can go on throughout life. And finally, I have to admit, although I would have hesitated while I was driving my Vehicle of Play to get all the necessary data and pictures, that it has been FUN, genuine RE-CREATION!

I'd like to invite the reader to jump in my Vehicle of Play or cruise along beside me. I feel I've only scratched the surface of what there is to know. Come along; there is much to be gained on the road ahead as one learns about living through PLAY!

Letters to Parents

When parents receive a letter telling about their child, that letter is often cherished, saved for the child's record book, or at the least, read with interest and a realization that they understand the child's world better.

Many parents do not understand the value of play; many do not realize the development which their child is gaining in play activities. It is hoped that these letters will give the teacher/caretaker some ideas for letters that can be sent to parents. The letter on page ??? may be copied and the blanks filled in at the appropriate places.

Note: The incidents in the letters are based on actual play experiences. The first took place in a group of children who were older four-year-olds and younger five-year-olds; the second was in a group of children who were almost three.

Dear Parents,

As promised in our introductory meeting when we presented our philosophy about the value of play, I'd like to share with you an incident from your daughter's play activities. Today Carrie was playing in the housekeeping area as she often does, and her friend Lance was playing in the block area nearby. Lance and another boy decided to build a launching pad for a rocket. Carrie and some other children joined them, but Carrie definitely showed leadership ability as she helped organize the play and assigned the "roles" each child was to fulfill in the building. She became very involved in the play. Carrie chose bricklayers and haulers and a "boss." She made the sign that pictured the rocket that would be launched. The conversation among the children was interesting and there was a real "give-and-take" in the speaking and listening among the children playing together. The kind of play Carrie was involved in showed several dimensions, each of which helps her develop in many ways. The *social* dimension of the play is called cooperative — you can easily see why. The *type* of play is generally called "symbolic." Carrie and her friends were using the blocks as symbols representing bricks and all kinds of equipment; they were also acting out different roles as they imagined them (and in this instance, as they had probably seen them on recent TV news). There were many *elements* of this play sequence, too. Carrie is gaining many skills of leadership in her play; that is obvious. She also is gaining prereading and writing skills as she made the sign (assisted by our aide, Mrs. Smith). Her communication skills are also developing rapidly.

We here at the _____ Center strongly believe that children develop in the most complete way when they are given the time and suitable environment to play creatively.

_____, Director

P.S. At our next parents' meeting, we'll show a video of some of the children's play sequences. This will help interested parents such as yourself understand the importance of play.

Dear Parents,

We thought you would enjoy hearing about an incident that took place as Clark was playing in our nursery this morning. Three children were in the housekeeping area; your son was in the midst of the play. "Let's make a BIG dinner," said Clark. "O.K.," said the others. Then they made a most fascinating feast, setting the table, cooking the food, etc. The observation that we found interesting, though, was that Clark freely substituted objects whenever a realistic play object was not available. (An example of this is that three types of blocks became three different dishes that the children needed.) This object substituation shows a definite progression in imagination and thinking skills. Sometimes we adults are so busy, we do not notice the progress that the child is making.

We at the _____ Center are committed to providing an environment and suitable materials so that each child can participate in many types of play. We know play is a medium whereby children can grow and develop in many ways that will help them live more effectively now and in the future. We are happy to share specific information about your son's play.

_____, Director

Dear _____,

We thought you would like to hear about your child's play activities. As you know, we are committed to providing an environment and materials so that each child can take part in many types of play. We are convinced that excellent learning and development take place during play and that you, the parents, will want to know about your child's involvement.

Following is a play incident in which your child participated.

_____

_____

_____
_____
_____
_____
_____

Some of the values that come from this type of play are:

_____
_____
_____
_____
_____

Some further ideas that we would like to share with you about the play activities:

_____
_____
_____
_____
_____

Sincerely,

_____, Director

Appendix B

Ways to Use the "List of Toys from Text and Illustrations"

1. Add your own favorite playthings to the list.
2. SAFETY! So important. With a group, analyze the list above. Discuss potential dangers. Are there any toys that are entirely risk free? If possible, go to a toy store and analyze toys for safety. Use your own knowledge as well as the markings on the packages.
3. With a group, decide which toys would be most developmentally appropriate for each of the following ages:

   • Infancy

   • Toddlers and Two-year-olds

   • Three- and Four-year-olds

   • Five-year-olds (kindergarten and after-school)

   • Six- and Seven-year-olds (1st and 2d grade and after-school)

4. Write briefly about a handi-capable child that you know. List toys that would/might be useful for that child. Then list toys that could be adapted and tell or draw ways that this could be done. If possible, check with a caregiver who works with the child.
5. You are a kindergarten teacher who believes that children learn about living through play. Some of your parents disagree; they are coming to see you. You will not be able to show a video, and decide that showing some toys and telling about the value that comes to the child as he/she plays with them will be most effective. Which toys will you choose? How could you get the parents involved in the discussion?
6. There are a few "playthings from nature" in the list above. Brainstorm with a group and list some others and the ages for which they would be appropriate. Talk about developing creativity by using natural and/or available materials.
7. Pugmire-Stoy has an evident fascination with playthings. Maybe your special interest is playgrounds. Plan a "dream" playground for various age levels. Now replan it so that it would be suitable for various types of handi-capable children.

LIST OF TOYS FROM TEXT AND ILLUSTRATIONS

airplane
animal figure

balance beam
ball and glove
balloons
balls (all kinds)
barrels
basket ball
beads
beanbag chairs
beanbags
bells
bicycle
Big Wheels
blankets
block accessories
blocks
board games
boards
books
bottle
bottle caps
boxes
brick
brushes

cameras
cans
caps
car
card games
cardboard boxes
cassette players
chairs
chalk
chart paper
checkers
clay
climbing apparatus
cockleburs
comb
commercial clay

cornmeal and steel bowl
costumes
craft sticks
crayon
cups
cushion

dinosaurs
discovery boards
doll carriages
dollhouse accessories
dollhouses
dolls
dominoes
dress-up clothes
drum
Duplo blocks

easel
envelopes
eye chart

glue

hammer
handbags
hats
household objects

inner tube (large)
interlocking blocks

jigsaw puzzles
jump rope

kitchen sets
knife, fork holder

laces
ladder
large needle

mike stand
miniature toys
mirror
mobiles

nature "media"
nesting blocks
newspapers
number cards

pails
paint brush
pan full of ice/snow
pans
paper
paper cups
paper plates
parent's shoes
parquetry blocks
pedal cars
pen
pencil
pets
picture book
pipe sections
plastic bottles
plastic containers
plastic lids
plastic shapes
play-dough
pots
pull-string toys
puppets
push toys
puzzles

ramps
rattles
rings on sticks
rocking boat
rocking horse
rope

sand box
sandpiles
sandtable
saucers
saw
scissors
screw toys
sleds
slides
softball
space ships
spoons
steering wheel
sticks
string

stuffed animals
styrofoam packing mate-
 rial
swings
switches (adaptive)

T-ball
teddy bears
teeter-totters
telephones —
 "911" teaching device
tennis ball
tin cups
toilet paper tube
toy auto garage

train
trampoline
tricycle
tri-play screen
toy trucks

waffle blocks
water colors
water hose
water table
wheeled toys
wood scraps
wood roller for marbles
wooden spoon

Resources for Toy Selection: Books

Auerbach, Stevanne. *The Toy Chest: A Sourcebook of Toys for Children.* Secaucus, NJ. Lyle Stuart, Publisher, copyright 1986.

Organized to provide information for making the best toy selection from infancy to age twelve. Each section of the book discusses the child's growth, needs at each age, and the most appropriate toys. Topics such as use of war toys, sexist toys, advertising, and other controversial issues are discussed in a rational, professional way to present the reader with facts and choices. Photographs, sketches, and excellent resource lists.

Cline, Victor B. *How to Make Your Child a Winner: Ten Keys to Rearing Successful Children.* New York. Walker and Co., 1980.

Chapter 4 ("How to Raise Your Child's IQ") has an interesting listing of toys entitled, "appropriate toys for various ages and growth stages."

Lederman, Ellen. *Developmental Toys and Equipment: A Practical Guide to Selection and Utilization.* Springfield, Illinois. Charles C. Thomas, 1986.

Excellent photographs. Classified by fine-motor, sensory, sensory-motor, and visual-perceptual development.

National Lekotek Center. *The Lekoteck Plan Book of Adaptive Toys.* 2100 Ridge Avenue, Evanston, Illinois 60204, 1987.

Includes plans for adapting existing commercial toys through the use of easily constructed home-made devices such as remote control switches and handle extensions which make the toys easier to operate.

Oppenheim, Joanne. *Buy Me! Buy Me! The Bank Street Guide to Choosing Toys for Children.* New York Pantheon Books, 1987.

An overview of the "buy-me syndrome." Selection of toys is by ages and stages through age eleven. An excellent directory lists resources, catalogs, etc.

Values of Play (as Pictured in the Vehicle of Play)

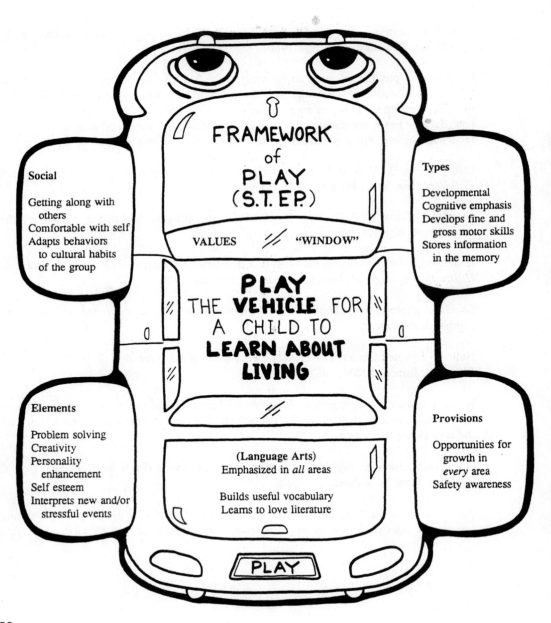

Social

Getting along with others
Comfortable with self
Adapts behaviors to cultural habits of the group

Types

Developmental
Cognitive emphasis
Develops fine and gross motor skills
Stores information in the memory

FRAMEWORK
of
PLAY
(S.T. E.P.)

VALUES   "WINDOW"

PLAY
THE **VEHICLE** FOR
A CHILD TO
**LEARN ABOUT
LIVING**

Elements

Problem solving
Creativity
Personality enhancement
Self esteem
Interprets new and/or stressful events

(Language Arts)
Emphasized in *all* areas

Builds useful vocabulary
Learns to love literature

Provisions

Opportunities for growth in *every* area
Safety awareness

PLAY

Bibliography

Accreditation Criteria and Procedures of the National Academy of Early Childhood Programs. Washingon, D.C.: National Association for the Education of Young children, 1984.

Allen, K. Eileen. *Mainstreaming in Early Childhood Education.* Albany, NY: Delmar Publishers, 1980. (in revision)

Belsky, J., M.K. Goode and R.K. Most. "Maternal Stimulation and Infant Exploratory Competence: Cross-sectional, Correlational and Experimental analyses." *Child Development* 1980m 51m 1168–78.

Brown, Roger. *A First Language: The Early Stages.* Cambridge, MA: Harvard University Press, 1973.

Bruner, J.S. *Child's Talk: Learning to Use Language.* New York: W.W. Norton, 1983.

Butterfield, Fox. "Why They Excel: What We Can Learn from Our Asian-American Students Who Are Winning Top Honors and Jobs." *Parade Magazine,* (21 January 1990): 4–6.

Chess, Stella and A. Thomas. *Know Your Child.* New York: Basic Books, 1987

Cohen, Stewart, and Gwenneth Rae. *Growing Up With Children.* New York: Holt, Rinehart and Winston, 1987.

Clarke-Stewart, A. and Susan Friedman. *Child Development: Infancy through Adolescence.* New York: Wiley, 1987.

David, Judy. "TV: When to turn it on — and off." *Good Housekeeping Child Care '88* (September 1988): 60, 86, 87.

Developmentally Appropriate Practice in Early Childhood Programs Serving Children from Birth through Age 8. Edited by Sue Bredekamp. Washington, D.C.: National Association for the Education of Young Children, 1987.

deVilliers, P.A., and J.G. deVilliers. *Early Language.* Cambridge, MA: Harvard University Press and William Collins, 1979.

Dunn, J. "Pretend play in the family." In *Play Interactions: The Role of Toys and Parental Involvement in Childrens' Development* (pp. 79–88). Edited by C.C. Brown and J.W. Gottfried. Skillman, NJ: Johnson and Johnson, 1985.

Elkind, David, "Giant in the Nursery — John Piaget." *The New York Times Magazine* (26 May 1968): pp. 25–27. A classic article that gives a "humanness" to Piaget, the theorist and appreciator of the individual child.

Elkind, David. *Miseducation: Preschoolers at Risk.* New York: Alfred A. Knopf, 1987. Pages 155–158 are a good section on play of five- and six-year-olds "when the balance of competence and helplessness is determined."

_____. "From Our President, PLAY." *YoungChildren.* Volume 43, #5 (July 1988): p. 2.

Ferris, Caren. *A Hug Just Isn't Enough.* Kendall Green, Washington, D. C. 20002: Gallaudet College Press, 1980. 0-913580-62-7. A photographic essay of deaf children and their parents' feelings. Interesting. Can be used as an example of books written about specific handicaps.

Frost, J.L., and B.L. Klein. *Children's Play and Playgrounds.* Boston: Allyn and Bacon, 1979.

Galinsky, Ellen, and Judy David. *The Preschool Years: Family Strategies That Work — From Experts and Parents.* New York Times Books, a Division of Random House, 1988. Chapter 2, "The Learning, Growing Child," (pp. 61–75) is very fine on play.

Gibbs, Elizabeth D., and Lynn E. Carswell. "Early Use of Total Communication with a Young Down Syndrome Child: A Procedure for Evaluating Effectiveness." Paper presented at the Annual Convention of the Council for Exceptional Children, 1988: ERIC EDRS Ed296 542.

Goodman, Richard, and Robert Gorlin. *The Malformed Infant and Child: An Illustrated Guide.* New York: Oxford University Press, 1983.

Hetherington, E. Mavis, and Ross D. Parke. *Contemporary Readings Child Psychology.* McGraw Hill, 1981.

Heward, William L., and Machael D. Orlansky. *Exceptional Children.* Columbus, OH: Merrill Publishing Company, 1988.

Hirsch, Elisabeth S. *The Block Book.* Washington, D.C.: National Assocation for the Education of Young Children, 1974. A classic collection of articles on building with unit blocks. Clear, meaningful illustrations.

Honig, Alice S. *Playtime Learning Games.* Syracuse University. Easy to read; popular book with parents.

Johnson, James, James Christie, and Thomas Yawkey. *Play and Early Childhood Development*. Glenview, IL: Scott, Foresman and Company, 1987.

Machado, Jeanne M. *Early Childhood Experiences in Language Arts: Emerging Literacy*. Albany, NY: Delmar Publishers, 1990.

Maccracken, Mary. *Turnabout Children*. Boston MA: Little Brown and Co., 1986. A private tutor's experiences with children with learning disabilities. Concludes with a creed for safe places "to work and play."

McKee, Judy Spitler. *Play: Working Partners of Growth*. Wheaton, MD: Association for Childhood Education International, 1986.

Miller, Karen. *Things to Do with Toddlers and Twos*. Telshare Publishing Co., 1984. Excellent ideas that stimulate play for this age level.

_____. *The Outside Play and Learning Book: Activities for Young Children*. Gryphon House. Copyright 1959. Mt.Rainier, MD.

Morrison, George S. *The World of Child Development: Conception to Adolescence*. Albany, NY: Delmar Publishers, 1990.

Musselwhite, Caroline R. *Adaptive Play for Special Needs Children: Strategies to Enhance Communication and Learning*. San Diego, CA: College Hill Press, 1986.

Nelson, K. "Social Cognition in a Script Framework." In *Social Cognitive Development: Frontiers and Possible Futures* (pp. 97–118). Edited by J.H. Flavell and L. Rodd. New York: Cambridge University Press, 1981.

Nicolich, L. "Beyond Sensor-Motor Intelligence: Assessment of Symbolic Maturity through Analysis of Pretend Play." *Merrill-Palmer Quarterly* 23, (1977): 88–99.

Odom, S.L., J.R. Jenkins, M.L. Speltz, and M. DeKlyen. "Promoting Social Integration of Young Children at Risk for Learning Disabilities." *Learning Disability Quarterly* 5 (4), 1982: 379–387.

Parent-Infant Curriculum: Home Training for Parents and Hearing Impaired Infants 0–4. Portland, OR: Good Samaritan Hospital and Medical Center.

Parten, M. B. "Social Play among Preschool Children." *Journal of Abnormal and Social Psychology* 28 (1933): 136–147. Reprinted in *Child's Play*. Edited by R.E. Herron and B. Sutton-Smith. New York: Wiley, 1971.

Partridge, Susan. "Children's Free Play: What Has Happened to It?" *Viewpoints*. 1988. ERIC EDRS ED 294 656.

Piaget, Jean. *Play, Dreams, and Imitation in Childhood*. New York: W.W. Norton, 1962.

Piaget, Jean. *The Origins of Intelligence in Children.* New York: International Universities Press, 1952.

Play as a Medium for Learning and Development. Edited by Doris Bergen. Portsmouth, NH: Heinemann, 1988.

Pugmire-Stoy, M.C. "The Secret of Having Fun: Nurturing Relations within the Family Structure." 7th Annual Proceedings, *Families Alive Conference.* Weber State University, Ogden, UT, 1986.

Pugmire-Weller, M.C. *Experiences in Music for Teachers of Young Children.* Albany, NY: Delmar Publishers, 1977.

Recchia, Susan L. *Learning to Play — Common Concerns for the Visually Impaired Preschool Child.* 1987. Available free from the Blind Childrens' Center, 4120 Marathon St., P.O. Box 29151, Los Angeles, CA 90029-0159.

Rogers, Cosby S., and Janet K. Sawyers. *Play in the Lives of Young Children.* Washington, D.C.: National Association for the Education of Young Children, 1988.

Roper, Annemarie. "Play and Gifted Children." In *Play as a Medium for Learning and Development.* Doris Bergen, Ed. Portsmouth, NH: Heinemann, 1988.

Schopsler, Eric, Margaret Lansing, and Leslie Water. *Teaching Activities for Autistic Children, Volume III.* Baltimore: University Park Press, 1983. Section 9 ("SOCIAL"), presents some interesting playful activities.

Segal, Marilyn. "Should Superheroes Be Expelled from Preschool?" *Pre-K Today.* (1987): pp. 25-27.

Sheridan, Mary D. *Children's Developmental Progress: From Birth to Five Years.* Windsor: NFER Publishing Co., 1973.

Singer, J.L., and D.G. Singer. "The value of the imagination." In *Play and Learning.* Edited by B. Sutton-Smith. New York: Gardner Press, 1979.

Spieker, Susan. "Study Links Tots Smiles." *San Jose Mercury News* 8 (13 September 1987).

Sutton-Smith, B. "The Play of Girls." In *Becoming Female: Perspectives on Development.* Edited by C.B. Kopp and M. Kirkpatrick. New York: Plenum, 1979.

Switzky, H.N., L. Ludwig, and H.C. Haywood. "Exploration and Play in Retarded and Nonretarded Preschool Children: Effects of Object Complexity and Age." *American Journal of Mental Deficiency* 83, (1979): 637-644.

Williams, Lois. "Horses and the Handicapped," *Soroptimist* 63, no. 4, (January/February 1990): 6–7.

Wilson, L. C. "Sounding Off!" *Pre-K Today* 3 (6): 51–53.

Wilson, LaVisa Cam. *Infants and Toddlers: Curriculum and Teaching.* Albany, NY: Delmar Publishers, 1990. Based on the CDA Competency Standards — excellent practical suggestions for any caregiver.

Index